SEASONS OF LIFE

prose and poetry for secular ceremonies
and private reflection

Seasons of Life: prose and poetry for secular ceremonies and private reflection
Compiled by Nigel Collins, co-editors: Jim Herrick and John Pearce.

First published in 2000 by the Rationalist Press Association, 47 Theobalds Road, London WC1X 8SP.

ISBN 0 30100001 8

Printed in Great Britain by Butler & Tanner, The Selwood Printing Works, Caxton Road, Frome, Somerset BA11 1NF

... How but in custom and in ceremony
Are innocence and beauty born?
Ceremony's a name for the rich horn,
And custom for the spreading laurel tree.

from 'A Prayer for My Daughter'

W. B. YEATS

CONTENTS

W.B.Yeats – inscription
Preface – Tony Harrison
Foreword – Nigel Collins

FUNERALS

WEDDINGS

NAMING CEREMONIES

PREFACE

Most poets spend their lives coming to terms in their work with what the editor of this anthology calls the 'seasons of life'. I have written poems on birth, marriage and death since I began to write. I wrote my own 'Epithalamium' for my first marriage and an elegy for the stillbirth of our first child. I have written poems to give support but not false comfort for dying friends and poems to commemorate their eventual and inevitable deaths. This has always seemed to me to be the area where there is the greatest need. As the compiler writes 'the greatest demand is at present for funerals'. I can't see that changing much.

The finality of death is different from the futures imagined for a married couple or a newly born child, though they too need their special commemorative texts and a sense of hope and possibility: that is the tone found in some of the texts included in this book. Often the suddenness of death gives little time for reflection on the most suitable texts. How often have I heard people wish for a large collection of possible readings to choose from. We have exactly that in this anthology.

Those friends and acquaintances of mine who know that I am both a poet and an atheist often ask me, especially when they have a funeral, if I can recommend a non-religious poem to be read at the occasion. And I've often tried to help by suggesting some of the poems in this anthology.

Even when I've given public readings of my own poetry and have included what are by now much anthologised poems about the deaths of my mother and father, I've noticed that they often make both men and women weep. Sometimes the people the poems have affected tell me afterwards that the words gave them a form for their grief, that they are unable to find in the traditional consolations of religious faith. And that is one of the great functions of poetry. My own grief is given a shape that allows it to be shared and to express the grief of those who read it to themselves or out loud at a public gathering. Poetry, at its best, tries to be more honest than religion. I have also written poems for a friend's committal and memorial, which I have read myself. Those who do not or cannot write their own poetry come to me for advice. This anthology has many of the texts I have also suggested to mourning friends, my favourite Edward Fitzgerald for example.

When I was making my film *The Blasphemer's Banquet* defending Salman Rushdie and the spirit of blasphemy, I was very happy to discover a grave in the vast Victorian Undercliffe Cemetery overlooking Bradford, which had chiselled on it the following stanza from the *Rubaiyat*:

> Lo! Some we loved, the loveliest and best
> That Time and Fate of all their Vintage prest,
> Have drunk their Cup a Round or two before,
> And one by one crept silently to Rest.

It stood out among all the other graves with their platitudinous pieties and it was wonderful to imagine it having escaped censorial Victorian scrutiny.

On my way to a recent showing of *The Blasphemers' Banquet* at the Aldeburgh Festival, I visited the grave of Fitzgerald in Boulge, Suffolk. Ironically the inscription on the translator's tomb probably had to pass the Rector's stern approval and he settled for a phrase from Psalm 100: 'It is He that hath made us, and not we ourselves'. But it has been suggested by his biographer that the praise was as near as he could go to a line translated by him from Persian: 'We are helpless – thou hast made us what we are'.

Although the text is Biblical, it has been suggested that it was merely his way of liberating the spirit of Khayyam from the Holy Bible. When a rose tree grown from a hip from the roses growing on the grave of Omar Khayyam in Persia was planted near Fitzgerald's grave the incumbent of 1893 was said to be 'dismayed'. The 'slow cultural process of liberation' referred to by the compiler means that we no longer have the problems which Fitzgerald had with the dismayed Rector and we are able to use our own texts.

Lucretius has also been a favourite suggestion of mine though his work still needs a great translation. I have also offered Marcus Aurelius about whom I wrote one of my plays. Research for that play led me to discover that the philosopher/Emperor often dictated his meditations while turning his gaze from gladiatorial combat or Christians devoured by lions, a context which, for me, slightly undermined his detachment. 'The Gate Afallen To' by William Barnes has also been a favourite, as has William Cory's translation of Callimachus and Cavafy's 'Ithaca'. Together with well-known favourites the anthology offers texts I am glad to be made aware of – lines like those of amateur poets like Barbara Castle on the funeral of her husband, with its tender sadness.

The anthology gives choices for all the seasons of life to suit many tastes, and bravely includes texts for suicide, like James Reeves' fine poem 'The Double Autumn'. It has many of the old stand-bys of rationalists and humanists, but also a generous and varied selection of modern poets and poets from lesser known sources. I am very glad that, when asked by bereaved friends for suggestions of poems, I can now refer them to this treasury.

Tony Harrison
Newcastle-on-Tyne, 1999

ACKNOWLEDGMENTS

Every effort has been made to obtain copyright permission for poems and prose extracts in copyright. In cases where we have failed, poets or publishers should apply to the Rationalist Press Association.

The compiler and publisher gratefully acknowledge permission to reproduce words from the following writers: Abse, Daniel (reprinted by permission of the Peter Fraser and Dunlop Group Ltd); Conrad, Aiken (from *Collected Poems Second Edition*, copyright 1953, 1970 by Aiken, Conrad. Used by permission of Oxford University Press, Inc.); Ariès, Philippe (from *The Hour of Our Death* by Philippe Ariès, translated by Helen Weaver, Allen Lane, 1981, reproduced by permission of Penguin Books Ltd); Armitage, Simon (*Zoom*, Bloodaxe Books, 1989); Auden, W.H. (from 'Twelve Songs XII' , *Collected Poems*, Faber and Faber); Belloc, Hilaire (Reprinted by permission of The Peters Fraser and Dunlop Group limited on behalf of: The Estate of Hilaire Belloc); Brittain, Vera (printed by permission of Mark Bostridge and Rebecca Williams, her literary executors); Caddy, Eileen (by kind permission of Findhorn Press); Campbell, Roy (*Collected Works*, Francisco Campbell Custódio, Ad Donker Publishers, 1985); Camus, Albert (from 'On Suicide' in *The Myth of Sisyphus* printed by Alfred A. Knopf Inc for Borzoi Books); Castle, Barbara (from *Fighting All the Way*, published by Pan Macmillan and permission granted by David Higham Associates); Cavafy (from *Complete Poems* published by Chatto & Windus); Churchill, Winston (from *Thoughts and Adventures* reproduced with permission of Curtis Brown Ltd, London, on behalf of the Estate of Sir Winston S. Churchill. Copyright Winston S. Churchill); Clark, Kenneth from *Civilisation* (published by John Murray Ltd); Cope, Wendy (from *Serious Concerns* published by Faber & Faber); Cornford, Francis (from *Collected Poems*, The Cressett Press,1954); Coward, Noël (copyright Noël Coward Estate and Methuen Publishing Ltd); Creeley, Robert (from *Collected Poems* 1950-1965 published by Marion Boyars of London and New York); E.E. Cummings (reprinted from *Complete Poems 1904-1962* by E.E. Cummings, edited by George J. Firmage, by permission of W. W. Norton & Company. Copyright 1991 by the Trustees from the E. E. Cummings Trust and George James Firmage); Day Lewis, C. (*The Complete Poems* by C. Day Lewis, published by Sinclair Stevenson [1992] copyright © 1992 and the estate of C Day Lewis); de la Corte, John (*How Can You Write A Poem When You're Dying of AIDS?*, by permission of John Harold); de la Mare, Walter (The Literary Trustees of Walter de la Mare, and the Society of Authors as their representative); Douglas, Keith (Reprinted from *The Complete Poems of Keith Douglas* edited by Desmond Graham [3rd edition, 1998] by permission

Collected Poems permission by Harper Collins Publishers Ltd); Read, Herbert (from *Annals of Innocence and Experience* published by Faber and Faber, permission by David Higham Associates); Reeves, James (by permission of the Estate of the late James Reeves); Santayana, George (*With you a part of me* published by Constable); Sassoon, Siegfried (Barbara Levy Literary Agency and Viking Penguin USA); Shaw, Bernard (From *Man and Superman*, The Society of Authors on behalf of the Bernard Shaw Estate); Shepperson, Janet (permission by Janet Shepperson ©) Smith Stevie (*The Collected Poems of Stevie Smith*, permission from Penguin 20th Century Classics and James MacGibbon); Spender, Stephen (*Collected Poems 1928-1985*, Faber and Faber); Stark, Freya (from *Perseus in the Wind*, John Murray [Publishers] Ltd); Tagore, Rabindranath (Publishing Department: Visva-Bharati, Calcutta); Tatchell, Peter (by permission of Peter Tatchell); Tessimond, A. S. (Autolycus Publications, Ltd); Thomas, Dylan (David Higham Associates Ltd); Thomas, Edward (*Collected Poems*, Oxford University Press and Myfanwy Thomas); Widgery, David (from *Some Lives* published by xxxxxx , permission by Sheil Land Associates Ltd) Wolfe, Humbert (© Ann Wolfe); Wright, Judith (*Collected Poems*, Carcanet Press Ltd); Yeats, W.B. (by permission of A.P. Watt Ltd on behalf of Michael B. Yeats, also reprinted by permission of Simon & Schuster from *The Poems of W. B. Yeats*: a new edition, edited by Richard J. Finneran. Copyright © 1983 by Anne Yeats); Young, Andrew (*Selected Poems*, Carcanet Press Ltd). Items by Fred Capuccino, A. Powell Davies, Donald Johnston, Kenneth L. Patton and David H. MacPherson from Unitarian sources.

With thanks to Shirley Dent for compiling the index.

INTRODUCTION

The rites of passage that form part of our culture existed long before the institutions where most people are used to seeking them today. Namings go back thousands of years, and wedding and funeral ceremonies are as old as humanity itself. All of them are shaped by a natural human impulse, present in the majority, to mark significant events in their lives with some kind of ceremony or ritual.

But there is nothing inherently religious about ritual. We all participate to some degree in personal and social rituals, whereas only some of us, and less than in previous times, voluntarily involve ourselves in religious rituals. The theological trenches dug to defend sometimes dogmatic interpretations of these events are now in the process of being breached; and for those who have become conditioned to automatically associating ceremonial with religious ritual, humanist ceremonies represent a reclaiming process evolving culturally.

Literature and music have likely always had an important role in ceremonial of all kinds. In humanist ceremonies, officiants and celebrants work assiduously, in conjunction with families to create a focus for celebrating a life concluded, with couples to reflect personal values in a relationship, and with parents who wish to acknowledge a *new arrival* in a meaningful way. However, on many of these both sad and happy occasions, it is ultimately an especially chosen poem or piece of music that has the capacity to move an audience and perhaps unlock their emotions.

Poetry, of course, has magical qualities, transforming mere collections of words into a heightened form of communication. It can often speak to traumatic or tragic bereavement situations in an oblique yet telling manner, and similarly enhances so-called *red-letter* days by finding a form of expression that rises above either the mundane or overly-sentimental.

In the course of the last ten years, during which I have conducted several hundred humanist ceremonies, predominately funerals but also weddings – conventional and same-sex – and namings, I have keenly sought suitable poetry and prose to offer for consideration on these occasions. In some instances it was not necessary to make suggestions, as my clients already had a clear idea of what they wanted included – and I first made the acquaintance of many of the poems and passages in this anthology in this way. Others I have been grateful to receive from friends and colleagues, for happily an ethos exists in the country-wide network of humanist officiants for sharing discoveries and spreading suitable and specific material as widely as possible. This provides for a communal acquisition offering easy access to a wide range of material – which in turn provides our clients with a very wide and varied choice.

The publication of *Seasons of Life* is part of this process, and the significant growth in humanist ceremonies in the last ten years or so has added to the demand for a book that, while as far as possible avoiding duplication with other similar anthologies, offers a substantial collection of humanist readings under one cover. While it will serve existing humanist officiants, and families undertaking their own ceremonies, in this very practical sense, hopefully it may also provide a source of comfort for the bereaved or a source of inspiration for those about to be wed – as well as contributing as a source of humanist thought and philosophy for schools and the wider public.

In terms of humanist ceremonies, by far the greatest demand now – as it will be in the foreseeable future – is for funerals. These take place for a much wider range of situations than generally imagined, catering not only for those obviously within the humanist atheist and agnostic traditions but also for those long lapsed from orthodox religious traditions, or whose marriages or liaisons may have created a religious divide.

In these or other circumstances requiring a neutral setting or greater degree of sensitivity than usual, humanist ceremonies, which while non-religious still have a capacity for reflecting cultural traditions or a spiritual dimension in the broader sense, can offer the most appropriate option. And many of the clergy now seem willing to concede that appropriateness is all where funeral ceremonies are concerned.

Funerals, whether structured as a religious service or humanist ceremony, are enormously diverse – ranging from crowded public occasions celebrating the distinguished or famous, to intimate small gatherings where the loss is no less deeply felt. I have conducted ceremonies where the palpable emotions of upwards of two hundred people have created a moving and memorable aura, and I am less often called on to officiate for very private ceremonies for just a handful of mourners. One such ceremony was attended by only a widow and her adult son; in their loss, her quiet dignity and his simple and unaffected reading of some verses from Chaucer, in honour of his father, were extremely moving – and the memory of it will long remain with me.

Diversity also applies to the circumstances of the death; while the majority of funerals are naturally for those who have attained their biblical 'three score years and ten' and well beyond, sadly there are also those for babies, children, and the young and middle-aged who have died before their time either from natural causes or in tragic circumstances of various kinds.

It follows from these examples of both very different scenarios and circumstances, that the range of poetry and prose to be considered for a humanist funeral should be wide and capable of satisfying a variety of tastes. There is a case for established and well-tried passages that have been found to be very effective for large public occasions, like Shakespeare's famous lines from *The Tempest* that begin 'Our revels are now ended'... and conclude ... 'and our little life is rounded with a sleep', or any number of stanzas from Edward Fitzgerald's translation of *The Rubaiyat of Omar Khayyam*, a work still much beloved by freethinkers everywhere.

Similarly effective are verses that have a musical quality or which demonstrate the function of sound in poetry, like the hugely popular *Remember* by Christina Rossetti or the extract from *The Joy of Living* by Ewan MacColl, its original and complete form being first conceived as a song.

There will be families or friends who for choice opt for Lucretius, Shakespeare, Hardy or Frost as a matter of course, while other households will veer much more to unembellished prose and even the prosaic for comfort. This anthology provides at least some examples of the former, including *What is Success* by Ralph Waldo Emerson, *The Journey of Life* by Winston Churchill, and two passages from the writings of Vera Brittain, who suffered much personal bereavement as a result of the 1st World War.

Similar consideration has to be given to the range of emotions to be catered for within a funeral ceremony. When saying farewell to those who have attained old age and whose lives have drawn to their inevitable close, considered meditations like those included here by Seneca, Montaigne, Bertrand Russell and Herbert Read can express the necessary sentiments. There are also passages, both ancient and modern, that express the acceptance of death in a serious but not necessarily sombre manner, and some modern poetry in a more light-hearted and even irreverent vein, like *Let Me Die a Young Man's Death* by Roger McGough and *Ivory* by Simon Armitage.

But, in the difficult circumstances of commemorating premature death more deeply felt poetry may be called for, and *How Long is a Man's Life?* by Brian Patten, *Dirge Without Music* by Edna St Vincent Millay, *For a Child Born Dead* by Elizabeth Jennings and *On the Death of a Child* by D.J. Enright are all powerful examples. Equally, there are ceremonies for circumstances like suicide for which the oblique quality of poems like The Road Not Taken by Robert Frost and *Heaven-Haven* by Gerard Manley Hopkins can be utilised in a positive way.

Other funerals still will be for subjects whose outlooks, ideals and examples in life are likely to have been widely respected or admired, and this can be tellingly reflected in the works of expressive writers like Robert Ingersoll or the inspirational poet Walt Whitman, in the uncredited *Humanist Credo*, or in poems expressing similar universal ideals, from different centuries, by George Eliot and Stephen Spender. Extracts like those included here by Thomas Paine – from *The Rights of Man* and Julian Bell, who at a young age was killed in the Spanish Civil War, reflect a political stance, while passages by the physicist Albert Einstein, travel-writer Freya Stark, and the unknown author of *Last Lines of a Materialist* are amongst those that speak for the many who, in life, possessed a clearly agnostic outlook.

For those departing for whom the natural world played a predominant role, readings about the countryside, gardens and wild-life, such as the few examples included here, can be entirely appropriate Equally, domestic pets often play an important role in people's lives, so we make no apology for including at least one cat poem, *Cats* by A.S.J. Tessimond, and *For a Good Dog* by Ogden Nash.

Finally, the predominant emotion often expressed at funerals reflects the love shared through life; the love expressed through marriages or partnerships, the love of children for parents – or parents for children, the love of relatives and close friends. Even just widely-held affection and respect manifested on public occasions can have a particular force, as regularly demonstrated by the highly publicised funerals of some public figures and celebrities. Hence the section titled *Love and Death*, which includes a range of poetry and prose reflecting human love and affection.

* * *

Though obviously different in tone from funerals, humanist wedding and naming ceremonies have a similar requirement from poetry and prose – that is to provide the necessary degree of both *gravitas* and humour, and to heighten the emotions with words beyond the mundane.

As for funerals, couples devising humanist weddings and parents contemplating naming ceremonies for new arrivals require readings that are wide-ranging in both tone and taste. There is perhaps also a greater opportunity than in the funeral situation to be imaginative or unconventional about the choice of material.

Given the plethora of anthologies of love poems, it might be thought that selecting items for a wedding ceremony would present no problem. However, prospective wedding couples who undertake the exercise of trawling through these compilations are likely to become disillusioned, as they discover that love poetry, as such, to be read aloud in public, is not necessarily a suitable choice at all!

There are exceptions, such as Shakespeare's immortal 'Sonnet 116', 'The Good Morrow' by John Donne, and two justly famous sonnets by Christina Rossetti and Elizabeth Barrett Browning, which are of such excellence and renown they transcend any possibility of being considered either overly-sentimental or somewhat indelicate. But much classical *love poetry* of lesser pedigree has the potential for all-round embarrassment at a public event like a wedding... not to mention strictly amateur efforts which, in my experience, however well-meant, rarely rise above the level of doggerel!

Fortunately twentieth-century poetry in particular provides some good but by no means florid examples of the genre, and assembled here is a selection which are by turns deeply-felt, *You are part of me...* by Frank Yerby and *The Confirmation* by Edwin Muir, passionate, *Strawberries* by Edwin Morgan, restrained and unpretentious, *Love Comes Quietly* by Robert Creeley and *Notes on Love and Courage* by Hugh Prather, and funny and quirky, *Valentine* by Carol Ann Duffy and *The Orange* by Wendy Cope.

For those wedding couples whose choice would in any case be for prose over poetry, there are a number of considered reflections on the art and nature of marriage, ranging from the eloquent, *It is not enough to love passionately: you must also love well...* by Anatole France and a passage from *Gift from the Sea* by Anne Morrow Lindbergh, to more prosaic offerings which nevertheless impart much good and timely advice, *The Art of a Good Marriage* by Wilfred Arlan Peterson and Paul Kurtz's thoughts on *A Successful Marriage...*

Weddings can cover a wide range of partnerships, including same-sex affirmations for which many of the included items are equally suitable.

* * *

With the ever-increasing secularisation of society there is enormous potential for the growth of humanist naming ceremonies, where parents wish to mark births with some kind of meaningful ceremony which, though neither over-formal or pretentious, *is* essentially serious in tone. Such a ceremony may just be the precursor to a party, but will nevertheless constitute a brief reflective interlude. It can also provide the framework for a symbolic act, like the lighting of candles or the planting of a tree, and for the appointment of those family members and friends who, by one name or another, will assume the secular elements at least of the important *godparenting* role.

Poetry and prose for such joyous occasions needs to reflect on the phenomenon of the birth itself, if not literally miraculous – then certainly wondrous, in poems included here like *Birth* by Langston Hughes, *The New Born* by C. DayLewis, and *Woman to Child* by Judith Wright. Then the hopes, aspirations and fears of parents for the future of their children are explored in the poems *A Prayer for my Daughter* by W.B.Yeats, *Born Yesterday* by Philip Larkin, and memorable prose passages from *The Firstborn* by Laurie Lee and the writings of A. Powell Davies and Kenneth L. Patton.

Last but not least, there are a selection of contrasting readings which acknowledge the inevitability and desirability of children growing away from their parents to forge their own identities and eventually live their own lives. Foremost amongst these are *The Gift* by the Indian poet Rabindranath Tagore, and *A Wish for my Children* by Evangeline Paterson.

*   *   *

While there was relatively little difficulty in accumulating for this anthology a wide-ranging choice of material for humanist funeral and memorial ceremonies, seeking out entirely suitable readings for humanist weddings and namings proved far more problematic. So the search needs to go on for imaginative and inspiring pieces for these latter two important social rituals particularly. But the discovery of further possibilities for funeral readings, whether reflective or consolatory, will be no less welcome, as there are now some famous examples, both religious and secular, in danger of becoming clichés through over-use.

Humanist officiants and celebrants encourage people to choose readings which speak to them personally. They may have first encountered such a poem or passage at a ceremony, or through a school assembly, a broadcast or a poetry reading, or in print. Many families and couples who have used humanist officiants and celebrants have introduced them to material which has later been gratefully utilised by others. Through this time-honoured process, the result, in these pages, is a collection of essentially secular literature, much of it with a genuine spiritual or emotional power, which can be drawn on for a wide variety of purposes, beyond the ceremonies which are its point of origin.

Many readers of this anthology will use it as a resource when looking for a suitable piece to read aloud at a ceremony. Reading aloud, especially in the large and resonant space afforded by most crematorium chapels or other large halls, calls for preparation and perhaps rehearsal in the presence of a constructive critic. The cardinal rules when reading at all humanist ceremonies, but especially funerals, would include being familiar with the text, reading slowly and carefully with great attention to the meaning, and above all not appearing intense or attempting to 'show off'. There is no merit in trying to 'act' – certainly poetry doesn't need supplementary emotion: it is better to be true to the tone of the piece and to aim for a straightforward and sincere rendition. Most of the selections in *Seasons of Life* retain the masculine gender of the original text. The compiler and editors recognise that, in public reading, it may be desirable for references to gender to be appropriate to the individual circumstances.

This anthology has been compiled for the existing range of humanist ceremonies. Other occasions are arising, however. Increasingly civic dignitaries are requesting non-religious inaugural or dedication ceremonies, where reflective readings expressing universal values and aspirations, but without any religious connotation, are both acceptable and welcome. (*Secular Civic Ceremonies*, a collection of texts and readings compiled by Carole Mountain, is available from the British Humanist Association.) Many crematoria that hold Family Memorial Services each year now seek to include humanist contributions. Rites of passage more prevalent in other countries and cultures, such as coming-of-age are taking place, albeit on a very limited basis, and ceremonies to reaffirm marriage pledges are now by no means unknown. Even ceremonies for divorce, undertaken in the required conciliatory spirit, might have some therapeutic value to children (especially) and other relatives faced with family fragmentation.

Whatever inventive and imaginative possibilites the future may hold, we must be allowed the hope that in pluralist societies both new and established ceremonial occasions will become manifestly more inclusive. For despite the differences in interpretation bestowed on the rites of passage that have evolved – and continue to evolve – as part of our culture, the occasions themselves are surely 'everyone's land'.

Nigel Collins

FUNERALS

BEGINNINGS

READINESS IS ALL

REMEMBER ME...

ACCEPTANCE

TIME AND THE SEASONS OF LIFE

THE NATURAL WORLD

LOVE AND DEATH

OUTLOOKS AND IDEALS

UNTIMELY DEATHS

SUICIDES

COMMITTAL POEMS

ENVOIS

BEGINNINGS

I was not and was conceived.
I loved, and did a little work.
I am not, and grieve not.

W.K. Clifford – 19th C. humanist
and mathematician

I was not. I have been. I am not. I do not
mind.
Epicurean epitaph

Is it so small a thing
To have enjoy'd the sun,
To have lived light in the Spring,
To have loved, to have thought, to have done...?

Matthew Arnold – from 'The Hymn of Empedocles'

But of this I still feel certain: that whether or not the spirit of man is destined for some unknown flowering in a life hereafter, the benevolence of the good and the courage of the undefeated remain, like the creative achievements of the richly gifted, a part of the heritage of humanity forever. As such they attain their own shining immortality, though it is not without tears that we see them pass from our individual experience.

Vera Brittain – closing words of her biography of Winifred Holtby, *Testament of Friendship*

… No man is an island, entire of itself; every man is a piece of the continent, a part of the main; if a clod be washed away by the sea, Europe is the less, as well as if a promontory were, as well as if a manor of thy friends or of thine own were; any man's death diminishes me, because I am involved in Mankind; and therefore never send to know for whom the bell tolls; it tolls for thee.

John Donne

Now the day has wearied me,
All my gain and all my longing
Like a weary child's shall be
Night whose many stars are thronging.
Hands, now leave your work alone;
Brow, forget your idle thinking
All my thoughts, their labour done,
Softly into sleep are sinking,
High the soul will rise in flight,
Freely gliding, softly swaying,
In the magic realm of night
Deeper laws of life obeying.

Hermann Hesse

The third of the *Four Last Songs* (1948) by Richard Strauss is to a setting of this poem

KNOWLEDGE

Men say they know many things;
But lo! they have taken wings, –
The arts and sciences,
And a thousand appliances;
The wind that blows
Is all that anybody knows.

> H.D. Thoreau

All things to nothingness descend,
Grow old and die and meet their end;
Man dies, iron rusts, wood goes decayed,
Towers fall, walls crumble, roses fade...
Nor long shall any name resound
Beyond the grave, unless't be found
In some clerk's book; it is the pen
Gives immortality to men.

> Master Wace – from *Chronicle of the Norman Dukes*

It would be nice to think we were departing to a congenial reunion of all those others we have loved who have died, waiting to welcome us to Hotel Eternity. Nice but implausible. What does linger is something almost more powerful, which is memory. It is the world which is given to us, as Cicero states, 'as an inn in which to stay, but not to dwell'. It is what we have done in life that lives on, not the trumped-up version of eternity which is worshipped in dank cemeteries and gravestone jingles. What we deserve to remember is real courage, not bogus virtue lauded at the funerals...

David Widgery – from *Some Lives!* –
A GP's East End

To plunge upwards is the way of the spark,
By burning up and out, even as we die
We shatter and dominate the nameless dark,
With our gold death – and that is my reply!
Humbert Wolfe

READINESS IS ALL

... Not a whit, we defy augury; there's a special providence in the fall of a sparrow. If it be now, 'tis not to come; if it be not to come, it will be now; if it be not now, yet it will come: the readiness is all.

William Shakespeare – from *Hamlet*

Death must simply become the discreet but dignified exit of a peaceful person from a helpful society that is not torn, nor even overly upset by the idea of a biological transition without significance, without pain or suffering, and ultimately without fear.

Philippe Aries – *The Hour of Our Death*, trans. Helen Weaver

A little while and you will be nobody and nowhere,
nor will anything you now behold exist;
nor one of those who are now alive.
Nature's law is that all things change and turn,
and pass away,
so that in due order
different things may come to be.

Marcus Aurelius

INTEGER VITAE

The man of life upright,
  Whose guiltless heart is free
From all dishonest deeds
  Or thought of vanity:

The man whose silent days
  In harmless joys are spent,
Whom hopes cannot delude,
  Nor sorrow discontent:

That man needs neither towers
  Nor armour for defence,
Nor secret vaults to fly
  From thunder's violence.

He only can behold
  With unaffrighted eyes
The horrors of the deep
  And terrors of the skies.

Thus scorning all the cares
  That fate or fortune brings,
He makes the heaven his book,
  His wisdom heavenly things.

Good thoughts his only friends,
  His wealth a well-spent age,
The earth his sober inn
  And quiet pilgrimage.

Thomas Campion

When you start on your journey to Ithaca,
then pray that the road is long,
full of adventure, full of knowledge...

... That the summer mornings are many,
that you will enter ports seen for the first time
with such pleasure, with such joy!...

Always keep Ithaca fixed in your mind.
To arrive there is your ultimate goal.
But do not hurry the voyage at all.
It is better to let it last for long years;
and even to anchor at the isle when you are old,
rich with all that you have gained on the way,
not expecting that Ithaca will offer you riches.

Ithaca has given you the beautiful voyage.
Without her you would never have taken the road.
But she has nothing more to give you.

And if you find her poor, Ithaca has not defrauded you.
With the great wisdom you have gained, with so much
experience,
you must surely have understood by then what Ithacas
mean.

> Constantine P. Cavafy – from 'Setting Out on the
> Voyage to Ithaca'

FARE WELL

When I lie where shades of darkness
Shall no more assail mine eyes,
Nor the rain make lamentation
    When the wind sighs;
How will fare the world whose wonder
Was the very proof of me?
Memory fades, must the remembered
    Perishing be?

Oh, when this my dust surrenders
Hand, foot, lip, to dust again,
May these loved and loving faces
    Please other men!
May the rusting harvest hedgerow
Still the Traveller's Joy entwine,
And as happy children gather
    Posies once mine.

Look thy last on all things lovely,
Every hour. Let no night
Seal thy sense in deathly slumber
    Till to delight
Thou have paid thy utmost blessing;
Since that all things thou wouldst praise
Beauty took from those who loved them
    In other days.

Walter de la Mare

HAPPY THE MAN

Happy the man, and happy he alone,

He who can call today his own:

He, who, secure within, can say,

Tomorrow do thy worst, for I have lived today.

Be fair or foul or rain or shine

The joys I have possessed, in spite of fate, are mine.

Not Heaven itself upon the past has power.

But what has been, has been, and I have had my hour.

John Dryden

11

... Death's a debt that everybody owes,
and if you'll last the night out no one knows.

Learn your lesson then, and thank your stars
for wine and company and all-night bars.

Life careers gravewards at a breakneck rate,
so drink and love, and leave the rest to Fate.

13

... Each new daybreak we are born again.

All our life till now has flown away.

What we did yesterday's already gone.

All we have left of life begins today.

Old men, don't complain of all your years.
Those that have vanished are no longer yours!

14

Life's an ocean-crossing where winds howl
and the wild sea comes at us wave after wave.

With Fortune our pilot, weather fair or foul,
all alike drop anchor in the grave...

Tony Harrison – from 'Palladas: Poems'

INVICTUS

Out of the night that covers me,
   Black as the pit from pole to pole,
I thank whatever gods may be
   For my unconquerable soul.

In the fell clutch of circumstance
   I have not winced nor cried aloud.
Under the bludgeonings of chance
   My head is bloody, but unbowed.

Beyond this place of wrath and tears
   Looms but the Horror of the shade,
And yet the menace of the years
   Finds, and shall find, me unafraid.

It matters not how strait the gate,
   How charged with punishments the scroll,
I am the master of my fate:
   I am the captain of my soul.

     W.E. Henley

DEAR LOVELY DEATH

Dear lovely Death
That taketh all things under wing –
Never to kill –
Only to change
Into some other thing
This suffering flesh,
To make it either more or less,
But not again the same –
Dear lovely Death,
Change is thy other name.

Langston Hughes

No single thing abides; but all things flow.
Fragment to fragment clings – the things thus grow
Until we know and name them. By degrees
They melt, and are no more the things we know.

Globed from the atoms falling slow or swift
I see the suns, I see the systems lift
Their forms; and even the systems and the suns
Shall go back slowly to the eternal drift.

Thou too, oh earth – thine empires, lands, and seas –
Least, with thy stars, of all the galaxies,
Globed from the drift like these, like these thou too
Shall go. Thou art going, hour by hour, like these.

Nothing abides. Thy seas in delicate haze
Go off; those mooned sands forsake their place;
And where they are, shall other seas in turn
Mow with their scythes of whiteness other bays...

The seeds that once were we take flight and fly,
Winnowed to earth, or whirled along the sky,
Not lost but disunited. Life goes on.
It is the lives, the lives, the lives, that die.

> Lucretius (Trans. W. H. Mallock) – from *On The Nature of Things* – *Book III*

TRUTH

Man with his burning soul
Has but an hour of breath
To build a ship of truth
In which his soul may sail –
Sail on the sea of death,
For death takes toll
Of beauty, courage, youth,
Of all but truth.

Stripped of all purple robes,
Stripped of all golden lies,
I will not be afraid,
Truth will preserve through death.
Perhaps the stars will rise –
The stars like globes
The ship my striving made
May see night fade.

John Masefield

Life in itself is neither good or bad; it is the place of good and evil, according to what you do with it. And if you have lived one day, you have lived all; one day is equal to all days. There is no other light and no other darkness; this sun, this moon, these stars, this order of things, all this is the same your ancestors enjoyed and the same that will welcome your descendants. And at the worst, the sequence and variety of all the four seasons, they embrace the childhood, the adolescence, the maturity and the old age of the world; the cycle has then played its game; it has no other refinement but to begin again; this will always be the same...

Whenever your life shall finish, it is then complete. The value of life is not in the duration; it is in the use; he has lived long who has lived a little. Give your mind to it whilst you are in it, it lies in your will not in the number of years whether you have had sufficient life.

Michel de Montaigne 'On Learning How to Die'
from *Essays* trans. Charles Cotton

... But death deserved or undeserved
is but eternal sleep,
dreamless and undisturbed,
and sleep comes easiest on a living day.
So let me be aware of living all the way
with no need to resent the fact
when life is fully spent,
able to watch it go with pride.
So let me now get used to life and death
and only put death aside.

> Kit Mouat – from the poem *A Matter Of Life And Death*

To me the Muses truly gave
An envied and a happy lot:
E'en when I lie within the grave,
I cannot, shall not be forgot.

> Sappho b. 612 BC

Greedy time feeds on all, harvests all, moves all things from their foundations, lets nothing last for long.

Rivers fail; the sea recedes and its shores become dry land; mountains are levelled and lofty cliffs come crashing down.

Such small events are barely worth a mention, the sublime firmament of the heavens itself will one day suddenly be consumed in its own flames.

Some time this whole world will be as nothing. Death summons all; dying is Nature's law, not Nature's penalty.

Lucius Annaeus Seneca

What if some little paine the passage have,
That makes fraile flesh to feare the bitter wave?
Is not short paine well borne, that brings long ease,
And lays the soul to sleep in quiet grave?
Sleep after toyle, port after stormie seas,
Ease after warre, death after life does greatly please...

Edmund Spenser – from *The Faerie Queene*

... If the world is not to last for ever, it seems to make no difference whether its time is to be counted in millions or billions of years; what matters is that there is an end. There can be no safe happiness until the fact has been faced and assimilated; and an absolute condition of all successful living, whether for an individual or a nation, is the acceptance of death.

How (the consciousness of death) comes matters little; but the existence of the vision of death gives life and beauty to this world. This is the happy reason that carries humanity singing across the dark ages; and those are fortunate who see it early so that they may enjoy a sense of proportion for the remainder of their days. An awareness of death is as essential in education as the study of happiness, or beauty, or intellectual enjoyment.

Whether or no it is accompanied by a belief in future life, appears to be less important. Unbelievers face their end as peacefully as Christians, and the fear of death is independent of rational guidance. It is a fear that in sickness comes closer, like a long wave shining in the sun; its immense ridge gathers unavoidable, a vanguard of the sea; and terrifies as it approaches, and towers with

facets of light over its darkening curve. But many that
have been under its shadow and watched it breaking and
felt its fear have suddenly known it to be no more than a
physical barrier, a mere reluctance in their departure
from familiar things; and tranquillity has come in sight
beyond the aimless foam. If one can hold to the
remembrance of such a revelation, one may hope to be
free for ever.

Freya Stark – from *Perseus In The Wind*

REMEMBER ME...

REMEMBER

Remember me when I am gone away,
Gone far away into the silent land;
When you can no more hold me by the hand,
Nor I half turn to go yet turning stay.
Remember me when no more day by day
You tell me of our future that you planned:
Only remember me; you understand

It will be late to counsel then or pray.
Yet if you should forget me for a while
And afterwards remember, do not grieve:
For if the darkness and corruption leave
A vestige of the thoughts that once I had,
Better by far you should forget and smile
Than that you should remember and be sad.

Christina Rossetti

Music I heard with you was more than music,
And bread I broke with you was more than bread;
Now that I am without you, all is desolate;
All that was once so beautiful is dead.

Your hands once touched this table and this silver,
And I have seen your fingers hold this glass.
These things do not remember you, beloved,
And yet your touch upon them will not pass.

For it was in my heart you moved among them
And blessed them with your hands and with your eyes;
And in my heart they will remember always
They knew you once, O beautiful and wise.

Conrad Aiken – from *Discordants*

THE DEAD

These hearts were woven of human joys and cares,
Washed marvellously with sorrow, swift to mirth.
The years had given them kindness. Dawn was theirs,
And sunset, and the colours of the earth.
These had seen movement, and heard music; known
Slumber and waking; loved; gone proudly friended;
Felt the quick stir of wonder; sat alone;
Touched flowers and furs and cheeks. All this is ended.

There are waters blown by changing winds to laughter
And lit by the rich skies, all day. And after,
Frost, with a gesture, stays the waves that dance
And wandering loveliness. He leaves a white
Unbroken glory, a gathered radiance,
A width, a shining peace, under the night.

Rupert Brooke

EPITAPH ON MY FATHER

O Ye, whose cheek the tear of pity stains,
  Draw near with pious rev'rence and attend!
Here lie the loving husband's dear remains,
  The tender father, and the gen'rous friend.

The pitying heart that felt for human woe;
  The dauntless heart that fear'd no human pride;
The friend of man, to vice alone a foe;
  For 'ev'n his failings lean'd to virtue's side.'

Robert Burns

... If it must be
you speak no more with us
nor smile no more with us
nor walk no more with us
then let us take a patience and a calm –
for even now the green leaf explodes
sun brightens stone
and all the river burns...

Martin Carter – 'Guyana'
– adapted extract from the collection *Poems of
Resistance* (1954)

They told me, Heraclitus, they told me you were dead;
They brought me bitter news to hear, and bitter tears
   to shed.
I wept as I remembered how often you and I
Had tired the sun with talking and sent him down the sky.

And now that thou art lying, my dear old Carian guest,
A handful of grey ashes, long, long ago at rest,
Still are thy pleasant voices, thy nightingales, awake,
For Death, he taketh all away, but them he cannot take.

      Callimachus (of Alexandria, c. 300-c. 240 B.C.)
      Translated by William Cory, 1858

SIMPLIFY ME WHEN I'M DEAD

Remember me when I am dead
and simplify me when I'm dead.

As the processes of earth
strip off the colour and the skin:
take the brown hair and the blue eye

and leave me simpler than at birth,
when hairless I came howling in
as the moon entered the cold sky.

Of my skeleton perhaps,
so stripped, a learned man will say
'He was of such a type and intelligence,' no more.

Thus when in a year collapse
particular memories, you may
deduce, from the long pain I bore

the opinions I held, who was my foe
and what I left, even my appearance
but incidents will be no guide.

Time's wrong-way telescope will show
a minute man ten years hence
and by distance simplified.

Through that lens see if I seem
substance or nothing: of the world
deserving mention or charitable oblivion,

not by momentary spleen
or love into decision hurled,
leisurely arrived at an opinion.

Remember me when I am dead
and simplify me when I'm dead.

                         Keith Douglas

Death hides no secret; it opens no door; it is the end of
a person.
What survives is what he or she has given to other people
– what stays in their memory.

                    Norbert Elias – *Love Lines of Dying*

FOR ANDREW WOOD

What would the dead want from us
Watching from their cave?
Would they have us forever howling?
Would they have us rave
Or disfigure ourselves, or be strangled
Like some ancient emperor's slave?

None of my dead friends were emperors
With such exorbitant tastes
And none of them were so vengeful
As to have all their friends waste
Waste quite away in sorrow
Disfigured and defaced.

I think the dead would want us
To weep for what *they* have lost.
I think that our luck in continuing
Is what would affect them most.
But time would find them generous
And less self-engrossed.

And time would find them generous
As they used to be
And what else would they want from us
But an honoured place in our memory,
A favourite room, a hallowed chair,
Privilege and celebrity?

And so the dead might cease to grieve
And we might make amends
And there might be a pact between
Dead friends and living friends.
What our dead friends would want from us
Would be such living friends.

James Fenton

AFTERWARDS

When the Present has latched its postern behind my
    tremulous stay,
    And the May month flaps its glad green leaves like
    wings,
Delicate-filmed as new-spun silk, will the neighbours say,
    'He was a man who used to notice such things'?

If it be in the dusk when, like an eyelid's soundless blink,
    The dewfall-hawk comes crossing the shades to alight
Upon the wind-warped upland thorn, a gazer may think,
    'To him this must have been a familiar sight.'

If I pass during some nocturnal blackness, mothy and
    warm,
    When the hedgehog travels furtively over the lawn,
One may say, 'He strove that such innocent
    creatures should come to no harm,
    But he could do little for them; and now he is gone.'

If, when hearing that I have been stilled at last, they
    stand at the door,
    Watching the full-starred heavens that winter sees,
Will this thought rise on those who will meet my face no
    more,
    'He was one who had an eye for such mysteries'?

And will any say when my bell of quittance is heard in
    the gloom,
    And a crossing breeze cuts a pause in its outrollings,
Till they swell again, as they were a new bell's boom,
    'He hears it not now, but used to notice such things'?

            Thomas Hardy

THE GOING

Why did you give no hint that night
That quickly after the morrow's dawn,
And calmly, as if indifferent quite,
You would close your term here, up and be gone
    Where I could not follow
    With wing of swallow
To gain one glimpse of you ever anon!

    Never to bid good-bye,
    Or lip me the softest call,
Or utter a wish for a word, while I
Saw morning harden upon the wall,
    Unmoved, unknowing
    That your great going
Had place that moment, and altered all.

Why do you make me leave the house
And think for a breath it is you I see
At the end of the alley of bending boughs
Where so often at dusk you used to be;
    Till in darkening dankness
    The yawning blankness
Of the perspective sickens me!

You were she who abode
By those red-veined rocks far West,
You were the swan-necked one who rode
Along the beetling Beeny Crest,
And, reining nigh me,
Would muse and eye me,
While Life unrolled us its very best.

Why, then, latterly did we not speak,
Did we not think of those days long dead,
And ere your vanishing strive to seek
That time's renewal? We might have said,
'In this bright spring weather
We'll visit together
Those places that once we visited

Well, well! All's past amend,
Unchangeable. It must go.
I seem but a dead man held on end
To sink down soon... O you could not know
That such swift fleeing
No soul forseeing –
Not even I – would undo me so!

Thomas Hardy

FOR A GENTLE FRIEND

I have come to where the deep words are
Spoken with care. There is no more to hide.
I toss away the cold stance of my fear

And move far, far out to be beside
One who owns all language in extremes
Of death. We watch the coming-in now tide.

We have lived through the nightmares death presumes
To wound us with. We faced the darkest place.
Death the familiar enters all our rooms.

We wear its colour. Its mask's on our face.
But not for long. It's good to let tears run.
This is the quick, the nerve, also the grace

Of death. It brings our life into the sun
And we are grateful. Grief is gracious when
It takes the character of this kind one,

This gentle person. We re-live his life
And marvel at the quiet good he's done.

Elizabeth Jennings

TAM CARI CAPITIS

That the world will never be quite – what a cliché –

the same again

Is what we only learn by the event
When a friend dies out on us and is not there
To share the periphery of a remembered scent

Or leave his thumb-print on a shared ideal:
Yet it is not at floodlit moments we miss him most,
Nor intervolution of wind-rinsed plumage of oatfield
Nor curragh dancing off a primeval coast

Nor the full strings of passion; it is in killing
Time where he could have livened it, such as the
   drop-by-drop
Of games like darts or chess, turning the faucet
On full at a threat to the queen or double top.

                Louis MacNeice

IMAGE OF A MAN

Into a tiny bay at Loch Roe, a tall yacht
groped, and anchored.
So many years ago. Why do I remember it?
Is it because of the tininess of the bay?
Is it because of the size of the yacht
and its sails fumbling down and furled?
Or is it because it was like a man I knew
who lived in the tiny village nearby?
A man splendid as that yacht, with a crew
of thoughts that were sad and merry
until the strange sails that carried him
fumbled down and were furled for the last time.

Norman MacCaig

THE LIGHT OF OTHER DAYS

Oft, in the stilly night,
    Ere slumber's chain has bound me,
Fond Memory brings the light
    Of other days around me:
        The smiles, the tears
        Of boyhood's years,
    The words of love then spoken;
        The eyes that shone,
        Now dimmed and gone,
    The cheerful hearts now broken!

Thus, in the stilly night,
    Ere slumber's chain has bound me,
Sad Memory brings the light
    Of other days around me.

When I remember all
    The friends, so linked together,
I've seen around me fall
    Like leaves in wintry weather,
        I feel like one
        Who treads alone
    Some banquet-hall deserted,

Whose lights are fled,
Whose garlands dead,
And all but he departed!
Thus, in the stilly night,
Ere slumber's chain has bound me,
Sad Memory brings the light
Of other days around me.

Thomas Moore

"... However far back you go in your memory, it is always in some external, active manifestation of yourself that you come across your identity – in the work of your hands, in your family, in other people. And now look. You in others are yourself, your soul. This is what you are. This is what your consciousness has breathed and lived on, and enjoyed throughout your life. – Your soul, your immortality, your life in others. And what now? You have always been in others and you will remain in others. What does it matter to you if, later on, it is called your 'memory'? This will be you – the you that enters the future and becomes a part of it."

Boris Pasternak– from *Dr Zhivago* (translated Max Hayward/Manya Harari – 1958).

SONG

When I am dead, my dearest,
Sing no sad songs for me;
Plant thou no roses at my head,
Nor shady cypress tree:
Be the green grass above me
With showers and dewdrops wet;
And if thou wilt, remember,
And if thou wilt, forget.

I shall not see the shadows,
I shall not feel the rain;
I shall not hear the nightingale
Sing on, as if in pain;
And dreaming through the twilight
That doth not rise nor set,
Haply I may remember,
And haply may forget.

Christina Rossetti

ACCEPTANCE

THE JOURNEY OF LIFE

Let us be contented with what has happened and be thankful for all that which we have been spared. Let us accept the natural order of things in which we move. Let us reconcile ourselves to the mysterious rhythm of our destinies, such as they must be in this world of space and time. Let us treasure our joys but not bewail our sorrows. The glory of light cannot exist without its shadows. Life is a whole, and good and ill must be accepted together. The journey has been enjoyable and well worth making – once.

Sir Winston Churchill – *Thoughts and Adventures*

IVORY

No more mularkey,
no baloney. No more cuffuffle
or shenanigans;

all that caboodle
is niet dobra. It will end
this minute.

No more fuss
or palaver; no more mush
or blarney. No flowers,

by request; no offence meant,
and none taken. No more blab,
none of that ragtag

and bobtail business,
or ballyhoo
or balderdash

and no jackassery, or flannel,
or galumphing.
Listen:

from this point forward
it's ninety-nine
and forty-four hundredths

per cent pure.
And no remarks
from the peanut gallery.

Simon Armitage

Mortal man, you have been a citizen in this great City;
what does it matter to you whether for five or fifty
years? For what is according to its law is equal for
every man. Why is it hard, then, if Nature who brought
you in, and no despot nor unjust judge, sends you out
of the City – as though the master of the show, who
engaged an actor, were to dismiss him from the stage?
'But I have not spoken my five acts, only three.' 'What
you say is true, but in life three acts are the whole play.'
For He determines the perfect whole, the cause
yesterday of your composition, today of your
dissolution; you are the cause of neither. Leave the
stage, therefore, and be reconciled, for He also who lets
his servant depart is reconciled.

Marcus Aurelius, Meditations

The delicate moments of time which mark our passing punctuate the present with such gentleness that it can altogether sheath from sight the blade of impermanence on whose edge we all live.

The loss of friends reminds us of the preciousness of time, the uniqueness of life, and the unrepeatability of personhood.

Anon

SNUFFING ZONE

Somewhere there is a driver
who killed our cat. Upset
at what had happened, ignorant
of which house in a London street
was hers, they laid her reverently
two doors from home.

"Shall I let her out?" I'd asked.
"As you wish," you said.
I found her stiff, unmarked,
a little blood and liquid on the stone,
caught leaping, tail outstretched
like the tiger in the ad.

Burying her in the territory
she'd ruled for two decades
we found a paving stone
we'd never known of,
as if in death
she'd led us to a new mystery.

Somewhere there is a driver
who saved our cat from death
by failing kidneys.
Now that I am entering the snuffing zone,
may I be let out on a warm night,
caught on the prowl for gossip, sex or power
and laid out reverently
and, dying, reveal another mystery.

Anthony Barnes

So death, the most terrifying of ills, is nothing to us,
since so long as we exist, death is not with us;
but when death comes, then we do not exist.
It does not then concern either the living or the dead,
since for the former it is not, and the latter are no more.

Epicurus – *Letter to Menoeceus*

The comfort of having a friend may be taken away, but not that of having had one. As there is a sharpness in some fruits and a bitterness in some wines that please us, so there is a mixture in the remembrance of friends, where the loss of their company is sweetened again by the contemplation of their qualities.

In some respects I have lost what I had, and in others I still retain what I have lost. It is ungrateful to reflect only upon my friend's being taken away, without any regard to the benefit of her being once mine.

Let us therefore make the most of our friends while we have them, for how long we shall keep them is uncertain. She that has lost a friend has the joy that she once had in him/her, to match the grief that s/he is taken away. Shall one bury the friendship with the friend?

from the Ethical Tradition

ACCEPTANCE

When the spent sun throws its rays on cloud
And goes down burning into the gulf below,
No voice in nature is heard to cry aloud
At what has happened. Birds, at least, must know
It is the change to darkness in the sky.
Murmuring something quiet in her breast,
One bird begins to close a faded eye;
Or overtaken too far from its nest,
Hurrying low above the grove, some waif
Swoops just in time to his remembered tree.
At most he thinks or twitters softly, 'Safe!
Now let the night be dark for all of me.
Let the night be too dark for me to see
Into the future. Let what will be be.'

Robert Frost

NO MOURNING, BY REQUEST

Come not to mourn for me with solemn tread
Clad in dull weeds of sad and sable hue,
Nor weep because my tale of life's told through,
Casting light dust on my untroubled head.
Nor linger near me while the sexton fills
My grave with earth – but go gay-garlanded,
And in your halls a shining banquet spread
And guild your chambers o'er with daffodils.

Fill your tall goblets with white wine and red,
And sing brave songs of gallant love and true,
Wearing soft robes of emerald and blue,
And dance, as I your dances oft have led,
And laugh, as I have often laughed with you –
And be most merry – after I am dead.

Winifred Holtby

And yet how I should prove that death is not to be feared, I cannot well tell, seeing the whole power of nature showeth that of all things death is most fearful: and to reason against nature, it were peradventure not so hard as vain. For what can reason prevail, if nature resist? It is a thing too far above man's power, to strive or to wrestle with nature, her strength passeth the might of our will, what help soever we take of reason or of authority: neither counsel nor commandment hath place, where nature doth her uttermost...

Thomas Lupset (1495-1530), *The Way of Dying Well*

LET ME DIE A YOUNGMAN'S DEATH

Let me die a youngman's death
not a clean & inbetween
the sheets holywater death
not a famous-last-words
peaceful out of breath death

When I'm 73
& in constant good tumour
may I be mown down at dawn
by a bright red sports car
on my way home
from an allnight party

Or when I'm 91
with silver hair
& sitting in a barber's chair
may rival gangsters
with hamfisted tommyguns burst in
& give me a short back & insides

Or when I'm 104
& banned from the Cavern
may my mistress
catching me in bed with her daughter
& fearing her son
cut me up into little pieces
& throw away every piece but one

Let me die a youngman's death
not a free from sin tiptoe in
candle wax & waning death
not a curtains drawn by angels borne
'what a nice way to go' death

> Roger McGough

NOT FOR THAT CITY

Not for that city of the level sun,
Its golden streets and glittering gates ablaze –
The shadeless, sleepless city of white days,
White nights, or nights and days that are as one –
We weary, when all is said, all thought, all done.

We strain our eyes beyond this dusk to see
What, from the threshold of eternity
We shall step into. No I think we shun
The splendour of that everlasting glare,
The clamour of that never-ending song.

And if for anything we greatly long,
It is for some remote and quiet stair
Which winds to silence and a space of sleep
Too sound for waking and for dreams too deep.

Charlotte Mew

DIRGE WITHOUT MUSIC

I am not resigned to the shutting away of loving hearts
   in the hard ground.
So it is, and so it will be, for so it has been, time out of
   mind:
Into the darkness they go, the wise and the lovely.
   Crowned
With lilies and with laurel they go; but I am not resigned.

Lovers and thinkers, into the earth with you.
Be one with the dull, the indiscriminate dust.
A fragment of what you felt, of what you knew,
A formula, a phrase remains, – but the best is lost.

The answers quick and keen, the honest look, the
   laughter, the love, –
They are gone. They are gone to feed the roses. Elegant
   and curled
Is the blossom. Fragrant is the blossom. I know. But I do
   not approve.
More precious was the light in your eyes than all the
   roses in the world.

Down, down, down into the darkness of the grave
Gently they go, the beautiful, the tender, the kind;
Quietly they go, the intelligent, the witty, the brave.
I know. But I do not approve. And I am not resigned.

Edna St. Vincent Millay

II

From a place I came
That was never in time,
From the beat of a heart
That was never in pain.
The sun and the moon,
The wind and the world,
The song and the bird
Travelled my thought
Time out of mind.
Shall I know at last
My lost delight?

Tell me, death,
How long must I sorrow
My own sorrow?
While I remain
The world is ending,
Forests are falling,
Suns are fading,
While I am here
Now is ending
And in my arms
The living are dying.
Shall I come at last
To the lost beginning?

Kathleen Raine – from 'Two Invocations of Death'

An individual human existence should be like a river – small at first, narrowly contained within its banks, and rushing passionately past boulders and over waterfalls.

Gradually the river grows wider, the banks recede, the waters flow more quietly, and – in the end – without any visible break, they become merged in the sea, and painlessly lose their individual being.

The man or woman who, in old age, can see his or her life in this way, will not suffer from the fear of death, since the things they care for will continue.

Bertrand Russell

Then a woman said, "Speak to us of Joy and Sorrow."
And he answered:
Your joy is your sorrow unmasked;
And the self-same well from which your laughter
rises oftentimes filled with your tears.
The deeper that sorrow carves into your being,
The more joy you can contain.
Is not the cup that holds your wine, the very cup
that was burned in the potter's oven?
And is not the lute that soothes your spirit, the very
wood that was hollowed with knives?
When you are joyous, look deep into your heart, and
you shall find it is only that which has given
you sorrow that is giving you joy.
When you are sorrowful, look again in your heart, and
you shall see that, in truth, you are weeping
for that which has been your delight.

Kahlil Gibran from *The Prophet*

TIME AND THE SEASONS OF LIFE

SONNET – THE HUMAN SEASONS

Four seasons fill the measure of the year;
  There are four seasons in the mind of man:
He has his lusty Spring, when fancy clear
  Takes in all beauty with an easy span:
He has his Summer, when luxuriously
  Spring's honey'd cud of youthful thought he loves
To ruminate, and by such dreaming high
  Is nearest unto Heaven: quiet coves
His soul has in its Autumn, when his wings
  He furleth close; contented so to look
On mists in idleness – to let fair things
  Pass by unheeded as a threshold brook.
He has his Winter too of pale misfeature,
Or else he would forgo his mortal nature.

John Keats

THE GATE A-FALLEN TO

In the sunshine of our summers
With the hay time now a-come,
How busy were we out at field
With few a-left at home.
When wagons rumbled out of yard
Red wheeled, with body blue,
As back behind them loudly slammed
The gate a-fallen to.

Through the dayshine of how many years
The gate has now a-swung,
Behind the feet of full-grown men
And footsteps of the young.
Through years of days it swung to us
Behind each little shoe,
As we tripped lightly on before
The gate a-fallen to.

In evening time of starry night
How mother sat at home,
And kept her blazing fire bright
Till father should have come.
And how she quickened up and smiled
And stirred her fire a-new,
To hear the tramping horses' steps
A gate a-fallen to.

And oft do come a saddened hour
When there must go away,
One well-beloved to our heart's core,
For long, perhaps for aye;
And oh! it is a touching thing
The loving heart must rue,
To hear behind his last farewell
The gate a-fallen to.

William Barnes

QUATRAINS FROM THE RUBAIYAT OF OMAR KHAYYAM

(20-23)

Oh, my Beloved, fill the Cup that clears
TO-DAY of past Regrets and Future Fears –
To-morrow? – Why. To-morrow I may be
Myself with Yesterday's Sev'n Thousand Years.

Lo! Some we loved, the loveliest and best
That Time and Fate of all their Vintage prest,
Have drunk their Cup a Round or two before,
And one by one crept silently to Rest.

And we, that now make merry in the Room
They left, and Summer dresses in new Bloom,
Ourselves must we beneath the Couch of Earth
Descend, ourselves to make a Couch – for whom?

Ah, make the most of what we yet may spend,
Before we too into the Dust descend;
Dust into Dust, and under Dust, to lie,
Sans Wine, sans Song, sans Singer, and – sans End!

(31-34)

Up from Earth's Centre through the Seventh Gate
I rose, and on the Throne of Saturn sate,
And many Knots unravel'd by the Road;
But not the Knot of Human Death and Fate.

There was a Door to which I found no Key:
There was a Veil past which I could not see:
Some little Talk awhile of ME and THEE
There seem'd – and then no more of THEE and ME.

Then to the rolling Heav'n itself I cried,
Asking, 'What Lamp had Destiny to guide
Her little Children stumbling in the Dark?'
And – 'A blind Understanding!' Heav'n replied.

Then to this earthen Bowl did I adjourn
My lip the secret Well of Life to learn:
And Lip to Lip it murmur'd – 'While you live
Drink! – for once dead you never shall return.'

from Edward Fitzgerald's translation (1859)

HEREDITY

I am the family face;
Flesh perishes, I live on,
Projecting trait and trace
Through time to times anon,
And leaping from place to place
Over oblivion.

The years-heired feature that can
In curve and voice and eye
Despise the human span
Of durance – that is I;
The eternal thing in man,
That heeds no call to die.

Thomas Hardy

AFTER THE LAST BREATH

There's no more to be done, or feared, or hoped;
None now need watch, speak low, and list, and tire;
No irksome crease outsmoothed, no pillow sloped
    Does she require.

Blankly we gaze. We are free to go or stay;
Our morrow's anxious plans have missed their aim;
Whether we leave tonight or wait till day
    Counts as the same.

The lettered vessels of medicaments
Seem asking wherefore we have set them here;
Each palliative its silly face presents
    As useless gear.

And yet we feel that something savours well;
We note a numb relief withheld before;
Our well-beloved is prisoner in the cell
    Of Time no more.

We see by littles now the deft achievement
Wherby she has escaped the Wrongers all,
In view of which our momentary bereavement
    Outshapes but small.
        Thomas Hardy

Cities and Thrones and Powers
　　Stand in Time's eye,
Almost as long as flowers
　　Which daily die:
But, as new buds put forth
　　To glad new men,
Out of the spent and unconsidered Earth
　　The Cities rise again.

This season's Daffodil
　　She never hears
What change, what chance, what chill,
　　Cut down last year's;
But with bold countenance,
　　And knowledge small,
Esteems her seven days' continuance
　　To be perpetual.

So Time that is o'er kind
　　To all that be,
Ordains us e'en as blind,
　　As bold as she:
That in our very death,
　　And burial sure,
Shadow to shadow, well persuaded, saith,
'See how our works endure!'
　　　　　　Rudyard Kipling

In my view death is simply one of the many kinds of tragedy that human beings encounter, yet unique because it is inevitable and universal. So let us not attempt to mask the tragic aspects of death, but not be preoccupied with it, nor allow it, on account of heart-ache and crisis it causes, to overshadow the other phases of human life.

Let us look death in the face with honesty, with dignity and with calmness, recognising that some unhappiness is inherent in human experience, but that together we have the resources to come to terms with this fact.

Corliss Lamont

PASSING STRANGE

Out of the earth to rest or range
Perpetual in perpetual change
The unknown passing through the strange.

For all things change, the darkness changes,
The wandering spirits change their ranges,
The corn is gathered to the granges.

The corn is sown again, it grows;
The stars burn out, the darkness goes;
The rhythms change, they do not close.

They change, and we, who pass like foam,
Like dust blown through the streets of Rome,
Change ever, too; we have no home,

Only a beauty, only a power,
Sad in the fruit, bright in the flower,
Endlessly erring for its hour,

But gathering, as we stray, a sense
Of Life, so lovely and intense,
It lingers when we wander hence.

That those who follow feel behind
Their backs, when all before is blind,
Our joy a rampart to the mind.

John Masefield

TIME

Time is the root of all this earth;
Those creatures who from Time had birth,
Within his bosom at the end
Shall sleep; Time has no enemy or friend.

All we in one long caravan
Are journeying since the world began;
We know not whither, but we know
Time guideth at the front, and all must go.

Like as the wind upon the field
Bows every herb, and all must yield,
So we beneath Time's passing breath
Bow each in turn, – why tears for birth or death?

from an Indian poem, 'Bhartrihari',
translated by Paul Elmer More

THE LAPSE OF THE YEAR

SPRING am I, too soft of heart
Much to speak ere I depart:
Ask the summer-tide to prove
The abundance of my love

SUMMER looked for long am I
Much shall change or ere I die
Prithee take it not amiss
Though I weary thee with bliss!

Laden AUTUMN here I stand,
Weak of heart and worn of hand;
Speak the word that sets me free,
Nought but rest seems good to me.

Ah, shall WINTER mend your case?
Set your teeth the wind to face,
Beat the snow down, tread the frost,
All is gained when all is lost.

William Morris

I HAVE A RENDEZVOUS WITH DEATH

I have a rendezvous with Death
At some disputed barricade,
When Spring comes back with rustling shade
And apple blossoms fill the air –
I have a rendezvous with Death
When Spring brings back blue days and fair.

It may be he shall take my hand,
And lead me into his dark land,
And close my eyes and quench my breath –
It may be I shall pass him still.
I have a rendezvous with Death
On some scarred slope of battered hill,
When Spring comes round again this year
And the first meadow flowers appear.

God knows 'twere better to be deep
Pillowed in silk and scented down,
Where Love throbs out in blissful sleep,
Pulse nigh to pulse, and breath to breath,
Where hushed awakenings are dear...
But I've a rendezvous with Death
At midnight in some flaming town,
When Spring trips north again this year;
And I to my pledged word am true,
I shall not fail that rendezvous.

Alan Seeger

... From too much love of living,
 From hope and fear set free,

We thank with brief thanksgiving
 Whatever gods may be
That no life lives for ever;
That dead men rise up never;
That even the weariest river
 Winds somewhere safe to sea.

Then star nor sun shall waken,
 Nor any change of light:
Nor sound of waters shaken,
 Nor any sound or sight:
Nor wintry leaves nor vernal,
Nor days nor things diurnal;
Only the sleep eternal
 In an eternal night.

   A.C. Swinburne – from 'The Garden of Proserpine'

LIGHTS OUT

I have come to the borders of sleep,
The unfathomable deep
Forest, where all must lose
Their way, however straight
Or winding, soon or late;
They can not choose.

Many a road and track
That since the dawn's first crack
Up to the forest brink
Deceived the travellers,
Suddenly now blurs,
And in they sink.

Here love ends –
Despair, ambition ends;
All pleasure and all trouble,
Although most sweet or bitter,
Here ends, in sleep that is sweeter
Than tasks most noble.

There is not any book
Or face of dearest look
That I would not turn from now
To go into the unknown
I must enter, and leave, alone,
I know not how.

The tall forest towers:
Its cloudy foliage lowers
Ahead, shelf above shelf:
Its silence I hear and obey
That I may lose my way
And myself.

Edward Thomas

Even as night darkens the green earth
the wheel turns, death follows birth.
Strive as you sleep with every breath
that you may wake past day, past death.

– from 'The Wheel Of Death', Ed. Philip Kapleau –
Writings from Zen Buddhist and Other Sources

THE NATURAL WORLD

IN HARDWOOD GROVES

The same leaves over and over again!
They fall from giving shade above,
To make one texture of faded brown
And fit the earth like a leather glove.

Before the leaves can mount again
To fill the trees with another shade,
They must go down past things coming up.
They must go down into the dark decayed.

They *must* be pierced by flowers and put
Beneath the feet of dancing flowers.
However it is in some other world
I know that this is the way in ours.

Robert Frost

'REGRET NOT ME'

Regret not me;
Beneath the sunny tree
I lie uncaring, slumbering peacefully.

Swift as the light
I flew my faery flight;
Ecstatically I moved, and feared no night.

I did not know
That heydays fade and go,
But deemed that what was would be always so.

I skipped at morn
Between the yellowing corn,
Thinking it good and glorious to be born.

I ran at eves
Among the piled-up sheaves,
Dreaming 'I grieve not, therefore nothing grieves.'

Now soon will come
The apple, pear, and plum,
And hinds will sing, and autumn insects hum.

Again you will fare
To cider-makings rare,
And junketings; but I shall not be there.

Yet gaily sing
Until the pewter ring
These songs we sang when we went gipsying.

And lightly dance
Some triple-timed romance
In coupled figures, and forget mischance;

And mourn not me
Beneath the yellowing tree;
For I shall mind not, slumbering peacefully.

Thomas Hardy

THE GLORY OF THE GARDEN

Our England is a garden that is full of stately views,
Of borders, beds and shrubberies and lawns and
    avenues,
With statues on the terraces and peacocks strutting by;
But the Glory of the Garden lies in more than meets
    the eye.

For where the old thick laurels grow along the thin
    red wall,
You'll find the tool and potting-sheds which are the heart
    of all,
The cold-frames and the hot-houses, the dung pits and
    the tanks,
The rollers, carts and drain-pipes, with the barrows and
    the planks.

And there you'll see the gardeners, the men and
    'prentice boys
Told off to do as they are bid and do it without noise;
For, except when seeds are planted and we shout to scare
    the birds,
The Glory of the Garden it abideth not in words.

And some can pot begonias and some can bud a rose,
And some are hardly fit to trust with anything that
    grows;
But they can roll and trim the lawns and sift the sand
    and loam,
For the Glory of the Garden occupieth all who come.

Our England is a garden, and such gardens are not made
By singing:- 'Oh how beautiful!' and sitting in the shade,
While better men than we go out and start their
    working lives
At grubbing weeds from gravel-paths with broken
    dinner-knives.

There's not a pair of legs so thin, there's not a head so
    thick,
There's not a hand so weak and white, nor yet a heart
    so sick,
But it can find some needful job that's crying to be done,
For the Glory of the Garden glorifieth every one.

Then seek your job with thankfulness and work till
  further orders,
If it's only netting strawberries or killing slugs on
  borders;
And when your back stops aching and your hands begin
  to harden,
You will find yourself a partner in the Glory of the Garden.

Oh Adam was a gardener, and God who made him sees
That half a proper gardener's work is done upon his
  knees,
So when your work is finished, you can wash your hands
and pray
For the Glory of the Garden, that it may not pass away!
And the Glory of the Garden it shall never pass away!
      Rudyard Kipling

Myself, my family, my generation, were born in a world
of silence; a world of hard work and necessary patience,
of backs bent to the ground, hands massaging the crops,
of waiting on weather and growth; of villages like ships
in the empty landscapes and the long walking distances
between them; of white narrow roads, rutted by hooves

and cartwheels, innocent of oil or petrol, down which
people passed rarely, and almost never for pleasure, and
the horse was the fastest thing moving. Man and horses
were all the power we had, abetted by levers and pulleys.
But the horse was king, and almost everything grew
around him: fodder, smithies, stables, paddocks,
distances, and the rhythm of our days. His eight miles an
hour was the limit of our movements, as it had been
since the days of the Romans. That eight miles an hour
was life and death, the size of our world, our prison.

Laurie Lee – from *Cider With Rosie*

Leave this world, Nature says, as you entered here. The
same passage which you made from death to life,
without fuss and without fear, make it again from life to
death. Your death is in the order of things: it belongs to
the life of the world.

Lucretius

FOR A GOOD DOG

My little dog ten years ago
Was arrogant and spry,
Her backbone was a bended bow
For arrows in her eye.
Her step was proud, her bark was loud,
Her nose was in the sky,
But she was ten years younger then,
And so, by God, was I.

Small birds on stilts along the beach
Rose up with piping cry,
And as they flashed beyond her reach
I thought to see her fly.
If natural law refused her wings,
That law she would defy,
For she could do unheard-of things,
And so, at times, could I.

Ten years ago she split the air
To seize what she could spy;
Tonight, she bumps against a chair,
Betrayed by milky eye.
She seems to pant, Time up, time up!
My little dog must die,
And lie in dust with Hector's pup;
So, presently, must I.

Ogden Nash

CATS

Cats, no less liquid than their shadows,
  Offer no angles to the wind.
They slip, diminished, neat, through loopholes
  Less than themselves; will not be pinned

To rules or routed for journeys; counter
  Attack with non-resistance; twist
Enticing through the curving fingers
  And leave an angered, empty fist.

They wait, obsequious as darkness,
  Quick to retire, quick to return;
Admit no aim or ethics; flatter
  With reservations; will not learn

To answer to their names; are seldom
  Truly owned till shot and skinned.
Cats, no less liquid than their shadows,
  Offer no angles to the wind.

A.S.J. Tessimond

DEATH IS NOT THE END

Death is not The End

But the beginning

Of a metamorphosis.

For matter is never destroyed

Only transformed

And rearranged –

Often more perfectly.

Witness how in the moment of the caterpillar's death

The beauty of the butterfly is born

And released from the prison of the cocoon

It flies free.

Peter Tatchell – from the anthology
How can you write a poem when you're dying of AIDS?

... For I have learned
To look on nature, not as in the hour
Of thoughtless youth; but hearing oftentimes
The still, sad music of humanity,
Nor harsh nor grating, though of ample power
To chasten and subdue. And I have felt
A presence that disturbs me with the joy
Of elevated thoughts; a sense sublime
Of something far more deeply interfused,
Whose dwelling is the light of setting suns,
And the round ocean and the living air,
And the blue sky, and in the mind of man:
A motion and a spirit, that impels
All thinking things, all objects of all thought,
And rolls through all things. Therefore am I still
A lover of the meadows and the woods,
And mountains; and of all that we behold
From this green earth; of all the mighty world
Of eye, and ear, – both what they half create,
And what perceive; well pleased to recognise
In nature and the language of the sense
The anchor of my purest thoughts, the nurse,
The guide, the guardian of my heart, and soul
Of all my moral being.

William Wordsworth – from 'Lines composed a few
miles above Tintern Abbey On revisiting the Banks
of the Wye during a Tour, July 13, 1798'

THE LAKE ISLE OF INNISFREE

I will arise and go now, and go to Innisfree,
And a small cabin build there, of clay and wattles made:
Nine bean-rows will I have there, a hive for the honey-
bee,
And live alone in the bee-loud glade.

And I shall have some peace there, for peace comes
dropping slow,
Dropping from the veils of the morning to where the
cricket sings;
There midnight's all a glimmer, and noon a purple glow,
And evening full of the linnet's wings.

I will arise and go now, for always night and day
I hear lake water lapping with low sounds by the shore;
While I stand on the roadway, or on the pavements grey,
I hear it in the deep heart's core.

W. B. Yeats

LOVE AND DEATH

And first an hour of mournful musing
And then a gush of bitter tears
And then a dreary calm diffusing
Its deadly mist o'er joys and cares

And then a throb and then a lightening
And then a breathing from above
And then a star in heaven brightening
The star the glorious star of love

Emily Brontë

I thought once how Theocritus had sung
   Of the sweet years, the dear and wished-for years,
   Who each one in a gracious hand appears
To bear a gift for mortals, old or young:
And, as I mused it in his antique tongue,
   I saw, in gradual vision through my tears,
   The sweet, sad years, the melancholy years,
Those of my own life, who by turns had flung
A shadow across me. Straightway I was 'ware,
   So weeping, how a mystic Shape did move
Behind me, and drew me backward by the hair;
   And a voice said in mastery, while I strove,
'Guess now who holds thee?' – 'Death,' I said. But, there,
   The silver answer rang, – 'Not Death, but Love.'

Elizabeth Barrett Browning – from *Sonnets from the Portuguese*

High love and flaming passion will fall prey
to time,
For the body's joy must temper as the body
leaves its prime:
And memory must weaken as we move to
stranger strands,
But oh! I shall remember the kindness of
your hands.

Barbara Castle – recited by her at the funeral of her
husband Ted Castle

ABSENCE

I visited the place where we last met.
Nothing was changed, the gardens were well tended,
The fountains sprayed their usual steady jet;
There was no sign that anything had ended
And nothing to instruct me to forget.

The thoughtless birds that shook out of the trees,
Singing an ecstasy I could not share,
Played cunning in my thoughts. Surely in these
Pleasures there could not be a pain to bear
Or any discord shake the level breeze.

It was because the place was just the same
That made your absence seem a savage force,
For under all the gentleness there came
An earthquake tremor: fountain, birds and grass
Were shaken by my thinking of your name.

Elizabeth Jennings

SONNET

When I have fears that I may cease to be
   Before my pen has glean'd my teeming brain,
Before high-piled books, in charactery,
   Hold like full garners the full ripen'd grain;
When I behold, upon the night's starr'd face,
   Huge cloudy symbols of a high romance,
And feel that I may never live to trace
   Their shadows, with the magic hand of chance;
And when I feel, fair creature of an hour,
   That I shall never look upon thee more,
Never have relish in the faery power
   Of unreflecting love! – then on the shore
Of the wide world I stand alone, and think
Till Love and Fame to nothingness do sink.
   John Keats

ETERNAL LOVE

We both knew it was time for you to go
and I, with dread, would face the emptiness,
the unremitting loneliness,
the unrelenting end.
Your eyes gave me that one last look
of love
and – so it seemed – of something more.
Its meaning I could not then comprehend.

And so you left I thought for good
but still that look remained.
And it was then I understood.
This was not to be the end at all.

Your body may have gone, it's true.
But bodies change from day to day,
new cells reborn as old decay
Not so that inner self that makes you you,
That changeless self lives on, lives through.

The love we share,
much stronger than mere memory that fades,
goes on and grows and floods back in cascades
And overwhelmed, my very being dissolves
to merge with yours again.

You're with me
when the dewdrops glisten at tomorrow's dawn
You're with me
when the sun's rays lift the veil of misty morn.
You're with me
when the thrushes greet the day with song.
I feel you at my side the whole day long.
When shadows lengthen
You're still at my side.

And when night falls
and sleep takes rein,
you're there once more,
close to my heart again.

John Lacorte – from the anthology *How can you
write a poem when you're dying of AIDS?*

At times like this
We may look through books
For the perfect words
To give form to our feelings,
Make the thing complete,
Set the matter at rest.
But in hours of searching
Each piece lies rejected:
Too precise, too difficult,
Too harsh, not relevant,
Implying what we do not wish.

But look into the grey, wide sky,
And the thoughts will come
Like this –
Remember me when I loved you most
And you loved me most:
Remember me when I was my bravest,
And when I did you right.
Then let that be our secret bond,
And just once let us rise in the morning
And enjoy the light,
And know that that bird in the mist
Is returning to the sun.

> David Lott

FOR THOSE ONCE MINE

With you a part of me has passed away;
For in the peopled forest of my mind
A tree made leafless by this wintry wind
Shall never don again its green array.
Chapel and fireside, country road and bay,
Have something of their friendliness resigned;
Another, if I would, I could not find,
And I am grown much older in a day,
But yet I treasure in my memory
Your gift of charity, and young heart's ease,
And the dear honour of your amity;
For these once mine, my life is rich with these,
And I scarce know which part may greater be, –
What I keep of you, or you rob from me.

George Santayana

TO_____

Music, when soft voices die,
Vibrates in the memory –
Odours, when sweet violets sicken,
Live within the sense they quicken.

Rose leaves, when the rose is dead,
Are heaped for the beloved's bed;
And so thy thoughts, when thou art gone,
Love itself shall slumber on.

P.B. Shelley

FRAGMENT: *AMOR AETERNUS*

Wealth and dominion fade into the mass
   Of the great sea of human right and wrong,
When once from our possession they must pass;
   But love, though misdirected, is among
The things which are immortal, and surpass
   All that frail stuff which will be – or which was.

P.B. Shelley

'SAYING GOODBYE TO MY FATHER'

Today, I am made of tears for you.
Some noisy, some still frozen.
But those tears
Shall not dissolve me.
In each one is reflected a moment with you.
When they fall –
The moments will stay
Glistening.

Gillian Woodward

OUTLOOKS AND IDEALS

Each one of us can help in the glorious task of rendering
some service to the family which numbers more members
dead than living. Each can offer an impulse of pity, of
mercy, of justice. Each can add a useful thought, a
cheerful and sensible word, a happy song, an effort to
express something beautiful. Each can contribute a little
bravery, a little wisdom, a little aim accomplished. And,
by reason of that little tribute to the general wealth, we
may enrol ourselves among the influences that will pass
from age to age in fruitfulness and blessing.

Anonymous – Ethical Tradition

A HUMANIST CREDO

Where shall the human spirit turn
    when ancient creeds are dead?
What shall our faith as fuel burn
    when all our Faiths have fled?

We trust the human spirit still,
    the tide that brought us here;
the sense of good, the human will
    to learn the way of care.

The way is hard and wrong is strong,
    but we shall triumph yet,
as more will join the human song
    to give, as much as get.

To seek the best in you and me,
    to share and care for earth,
to serve a new humanity
    and bring world peace to birth.

    Anonymous – Ethical Tradition

Like nearly all the intellectuals of this generation, we are fundamentally political in thought and action: this more than anything else marks the difference between us and our elders. Being socialist for us means being rationalist, common-sense, empirical; means a very firm extrovert, practical commonplace sense of exterior reality. It means turning away from mysticisms, fantasies, escapes into the inner life. We think of the world first and foremost as the place where other people live, as the scene of crisis and poverty, the probable scene of revolution and war: we think more about the practical solution of the real contradictions of the real world than possible discoveries in some other world.

Julian Bell

I believe that order is better than chaos, creation better
than destruction. I prefer gentleness to violence,
forgiveness to vendetta. On the whole I think knowledge
is better than ignorance, and I am sure that human
sympathy is more valuable than ideology. I believe that
in spite of the recent triumphs of science, men haven't
changed much in the last two thousand years; and in
consequence we must still try to learn from history.
History is ourselves... I believe in courtesy, the ritual by
which we avoid hurting other people's feelings by
satisfying our own egos. And I think we should
remember we are part of the great whole, which for
convenience we call nature. All living things are our
brothers and sisters. Above all, I believe in the God-given
genius of certain individuals, and I value a society that
makes their existence possible.

Sir Kenneth Clarke – from *Civilisation – a Personal View*

THE RELIGIOUSNESS OF SCIENCE

You will hardly find one among the profounder sort of scientific minds without a peculiar religious feeling of his own. But it is different from the religion of the naive man. For the latter God is a being from whose care one hopes to benefit and whose punishment one fears; a sublimation of a feeling similar to that of a child for its father, a being to whom one stands to some extent in a personal relation, however deeply it may be tinged with awe.

But the scientist is possessed by the sense of universal causation. The future, to him, is every whit as necessary and determined as the past. There is nothing divine about morality, it is a purely human affair. His religious feeling takes the form of a rapturous amazement at the harmony of natural law, which reveals an intelligence of such superiority that, compared with it, all the systematic thinking and acting of human beings is an utterly insignificant reflection. This feeling is the guiding principle of his life and work, in so far as he succeeds in keeping himself from the shackles of selfish desire. It is beyond question closely akin to that which has possessed the religious geniuses of all ages.

Albert Einstein – from the English translation of
Mein Weltbild (The World As I See It)

O may I join the choir invisible
Of those immortal dead who live again
In minds made better by their presence: live
In pulses stirred to generosity,
In deeds of daring rectitude, in scorn
For miserable aims that end with self,
In thoughts sublime that pierce the night like stars,
And with their mild persistence urge man's search
To vaster issues...

                This is the life to come,
Which martyred men have made more glorious
For us who strive to follow. May I reach
That purest heaven, be to other souls
The cup of strength in some great agony,
Enkindle generous ardour, feed pure love,
Beget the smiles that have no cruelty –
Be the sweet presence of a good diffused,
And in the diffusion ever more intense.
So shall I join the choir invisible
Whose music is the gladness of the world.
             George Eliot

THE CREED OF SCIENCE

To love justice; to long for the right; to love mercy; to
pity the suffering; to assist the weak; to forget wrongs,
and remember benefits. To love the truth; to be sincere; to
utter honest words; to love liberty; to wage relentless war
against slavery in all its forms. To love wife, and child,
and friend; to make a happy home; to love the beautiful
in art, in nature; to cultivate the mind; to be familiar with
the mighty thoughts that genius has expressed; the noble
deeds of all the world; to cultivate courage and
cheerfulness; to make others happy; to fill life with the
splendour of generous deeds; the warmth of loving
words; to discard error; to destroy prejudice; to receive
new truths with gladness; to cultivate hope; to see the
calm beyond the storm; the dawn beyond the night; to do
the best that can be done, and then to be resigned...

Robert G. Ingersoll

Man's dearest possession is life, and since it is given to him to live but once he must therefore live as to feel no torturing regrets for years without purpose, never know the burning shame of a mean and petty past, so live that in dying he will say, "All my life and all my strength were given to the finest cause in all the world, the fight for the liberation of mankind."

Nikolai Alekseyevich Ostrovski – from *How the Steel Was Tempered*

All men dream: but not equally. Those who dream by night in the dusty recesses of their minds, wake in the day to find that it was vanity: but the dreamers of the day are dangerous men, for they may act their dreams with open eyes, to make it possible.

T.E. Lawrence – from *The Seven Pillars of Wisdom*

THE LIFE OF A MAN

Man belongs to the earth and to the planetary system of the sun. He is part of all the life of the earth. As the years have passed one after another, a million years after a million years, evolution has changed life's forms. Each form of life is sustained by many others and one form has been the source of another. Man is nature's most recent heir and his inheritance is his brain by which he knows what he is and understands what has made him what he is.

We are all, each one of us, a part of all the life which has gone before us and all that will come after us. Each life plays its own part in the history of man. Each one by his existence and by his activity plays a part in sustaining the life of mankind, and by his thoughts and his speech helps in maintaining the wisdom and the knowledge that men have accumulated ready to be passed on to the generations of the future.

Some men have made great additions to the knowledge and the skills of men. The contributions of some to the inheritance of mankind have been much greater than that of others, but we can never say that the effects of any life, however unseen they may be, are nothing. Day by day each life affects many others; the ripples from the existence of one pass outwards touching and shaping the lives of many both known and unknown.

Each man is himself, unique. We are all men, born in the same way, living, thinking, feeling, by the processes of energy within us, and yet these processes have the possibility of such variation that there are no two men alike. We have each something of our own to add to the life of man which no one else could give.

This separateness and uniqueness of man is the source of our sorrow and grief. Look through the whole earth and the one we have lost is not to be found; there is none like him. But he played his part in our lives; what he was still lives in our minds. Our lives which are a part of his life goes on and the ripples of his life are still passing outward in known and unknown ways. With those present, with those who have gone and with those who are yet to be born, he has his place in the procession of humankind and the process of life.

Margaret Laws Smith

OF SOCIETY AND CIVILISATION

Great part of that order which reigns among mankind is not the effect of Government. It has its origin in the principles of society and the natural constitution of man. It existed prior to Government, and would exist if the formality of Government was abolished. The mutual dependence and reciprocal interest which man has upon man, and all the parts of a civilised community upon each other, create that great chain of connection which holds it together. The landholder, the farmer, the manufacturer, the tradesmen, and every occupation, prospers by the aid which each receives from the other, and from the whole. Common interest regulates their concerns, and forms their law; and the laws which common usage ordains, have a greater influence than the laws of Government. In fine, society performs for itself almost everything which is ascribed to Government.

To understand the nature and quantity of Government proper for man, it is necessary to attend to his character. As nature created him for social life, she fitted him for the stations she intended. In all cases she made his natural wants greater than his individual powers. No one man is capable, without the aid of society, of supplying his own wants; and those wants, acting upon every individual, impel the whole of them into society, as naturally as gravitation acts to a centre.

But she has gone further. She has not only forced man into society by a diversity of wants which the reciprocal aid of each other can supply, but she has implanted in him a system of social affections, which though not necessary to his existence, are essential to his happiness. There is no period in life when this love for society ceases to act. It begins and ends with our being.

Thomas Paine – from *Rights of Man*

THE TREE OF LIFE

My own attitude towards death has never been one of
fear... My favourite symbol is the Tree of Life. The
human race is the trunk and branches of this tree, and
individual men are the leaves, which appear one season,
flourish for a summer, and then die. I am like a leaf of
this tree, and one day I shall decay and fall, and become
a pinch of compost about its roots. But meanwhile I am
conscious of the tree's flowing sap and steadfast strength.
Deep down in my consciousness is the consciousness of a
collective life, a life of which I am a part, and to which
I contribute a minute but unique extension. When I die
and fall, the tree remains, nourished to some small
degree by my brief manifestation of life. Millions of
leaves have preceded me and millions will follow me;
the tree itself grows and endures.

Herbert Read – from *The Falcon and the Dove*

Those who live nobly, if in their day they live obscurely, need not fear that they have lived in vain. Something radiates from their lives, some light that shows the way to their friends, their neighbours, perhaps to long future ages.

The individual, if he is filled with love of mankind, with breadth of vision, with courage, and with endurance, can do a great deal.

Bertrand Russell

This is the true joy of life: the being used for a purpose recognised by yourself as a mighty one; the being thoroughly worn out before you are thrown on the scrap heap; the being a force of Nature instead of a feverish selfish little clod of ailments and grievances complaining that the world will not devote itself to making you happy.

George Bernard Shaw

THE TRULY GREAT

I think continually of those who were truly great.
Who, from the womb, remembered the soul's history
Through corridors of light, where the hours are suns
Endless and singing. Whose lovely ambition
Was that their lips, still touched with fire,
Should tell of the Spirit clothed from head to foot in song.
And who hoarded from the Spring branches
The desires falling across their bodies like blossoms.

What is precious is never to forget
The essential delight of the blood drawn from ageless
    springs
Breaking through rocks in worlds before our earth.
Never to deny its pleasure in the morning simple light
Nor its grave evening demand for love.
Never to allow gradually the traffic to smother
With noise and fog the flowering of the spirit.

Near the snow, near the sun, in the highest fields,
See how the names are fêted by the waving grass
And by the streamers of white cloud
And whispers of wind in the listening sky.
The names of those who in their lives fought for life
Who wore at their hearts the fire's centre.
Born of the sun, they travelled a short while towards
    the sun
And left the vivid air signed with their honour.

                    Stephen Spender

A LOFTIER RACE

These things shall be, – a loftier race
Than e'er the world hath known shall rise
With flame of freedom in their souls,
And light of knowledge in their eyes.

They shall be gentle, brave and strong
To spill no drop of blood, but dare
All that may plant man's lordship firm
On earth, and fire, and sea, and air.

They shall be simple in their homes,
And splendid in their public ways,
Filling the mansions of the state
With music and with hymns of praise.

Nation with nation, land with land,
Unarmed shall live as comrades free;
In every heart and brain shall throb
The pulse of one fraternity.

New arts shall bloom of loftier mould,
And mightier music fill the skies,
And every life shall be a song
When all the earth is paradise.

John Addington Symonds

This life is short, the
vanities of the world are
transient; they alone live
who live for others, the
rest are more dead than
alive.

Swami Vivekananda

... This is what you shall do: Love the earth and sun and
the animals, despise riches, give alms to everyone that
asks, stand up for the stupid and crazy, devote your
income and labor to others, hate tyrants, argue not
concerning God, have patience and indulgence towards
the people, take off your hat to nothing known or
unknown or to any man or number of men, go freely
with powerful uneducated persons and with the young
and with the mothers of families... re-examine all you
have been told in church or in any book, dismiss
whatever insults your soul, and your very flesh shall be a
great poem and have the richest fluency not only in its
words but in the silent lines of its lips and face and
between the lashes of your eyes and in every motion and
joint of your body...

Walt Whitman – from the Preface to
Leaves of Grass, 1855

UNTIMELY DEATHS

It is not growing like a tree
In bulk, doth make man better be;
Or standing long an oak, three hundred year,
To fall a log at last, dry, bald, and sere:
A lily of a day
Is fairer far in May,
Although it fall and die that night,
It was the plant and flower of light.
In small proportions we just beauty see
And in short measures life may perfect be.

Ben Jonson – from 'To the Immortal Memory and
Friendship of that Noble Pair, Sir Lucius Cary and
Sir Henry Morison'

THE ORIGIN OF MUSIC

When I was a medical student
I stole two femurs of a baby
from The Pathology Specimen room.
Now I keep them in my pocket,
the right femur and the left femur.
Like a boy scout, I'm prepared.
For what can one say to a neighbour
when his wife dies? 'Sorry'?
Or when a friend's sweet child
suffers leukaemia? 'Condolences'?
No, if I should meet either friend
or stricken neighbour in the street
and he should tell me, whisper to me
his woeful, intimate news,
wordless I take the two small femurs
from out of my pocket sadly
and play them like castanets.

Dannie Abse – from *Remembrance of Crimes Past*

I don't think that victory over death is anything so
superficial as a person fulfilling their normal span of life.
It can be twofold; a victory over death for the man –
who faces it for himself – without fear, and a victory by
those who, loving him, know that death is a little thing
compared with the fact that he lived, and was the kind
of person he was.

> Vera Brittain

His laughter was better than birds in the morning, his smile
Turned the edge of the wind, his memory
Disarms death and charms the surly grave.
Early he went to bed, too early we
Saw his light put out; yet we could not grieve
More than a little while,
For he lives in the earth around us, laughs from the sky.

> C. Day Lewis – from *A Time to Dance:*
> In memory of L.P. Hedges

ON THE DEATH OF A CHILD

The greatest griefs shall find themselves inside the
   smallest cage.
It's only then that we can hope to tame their rage,
The monsters we must live with. For it will not do
To hiss humanity because one human threw
Us out of heart and home. Or part

At odds with life because one baby failed to live.
Indeed, as little as its subject, is the wreath we give –

The big words fail to fit. Like giant boxes
Round small bodies. Taking up improper room,
Where so much withering is, and so much bloom.

                    D.J. Enright

NOTHING GOLD CAN STAY

    Nature's first green is gold,
    Her hardest hue to hold.
    Her early leaf's a flower;
    But only so an hour.
    Then leaf subsides to leaf.
    So Eden sank to grief,
    So dawn goes down to day.
    Nothing gold can stay.

                Robert Frost

Fair daffodils, we weep to see
  You haste away so soon;
As yet the early-rising sun
  Has not attained his noon.
    Stay, stay
  Until the hasting day
    Has run
  But to the evensong;
And, having prayed together, we
  Will go with you along.

We have short time to stay as you,
  We have as short a spring;
As quick a growth to meet decay,
  As you, or anything.
    We die
  As your hours do, and dry
    Away
  Like to the summer's rain;
Or as the pearls of morning's dew,
  Ne'er to be found again.
    Robert Herrick

FOR A CHILD BORN DEAD

What ceremony can we fit
You into now? If you had come
Out of a warm and noisy room
To this, there'd be an opposite
For us to know you by. We could
Imagine you in lively mood

And then look at the other side,
The mood drawn out of you, the breath
Defeated by the power of death.
But we have never seen you stride
Ambitiously the world we know.
You could not come and yet you go.
But there is nothing now to mar
Your clear refusal of our world.
Not in our memories can we mould
You or distort your character.
Then all our consolation is
That grief can be as pure as this.

Elizabeth Jennings

HOW LONG IS A MAN'S LIFE?

[Cuanto vive el hombre por fin? Vive mil dias o uno solo?
Una Semena o varios siglos? Por cuanto tiempo muere el hombre?
Que quiere decir "para siempre"?]
    – Pablo Neruda

How long does a man live, after all?
A thousand days, or only one?
One week, or a few centuries?
How long does a man spend living or dying
and what do we mean when we say, gone forever?

       *   *   *

Adrift in such preoccupations, we seek clarification.
We can go to the philosophers,
but they will weary of our questions.
We can go to the priests and rabbis,
but they might be too busy with administrations.

So, how long does a man live, after all?
And how much does he live while he lives?
We fret, and ask so many questions –
then when it comes to us
the answer is so simple after all.

A man lives for as long as we carry him inside us,
for as long as we carry the harvest of his dreams,
for as long as we ourselves live
holding memories in common, a man lives.

His lover will carry his man's scent, his touch;
his children will carry the weight of his love.
One friend will carry his arguments,
another will hum his favourite tunes,
another will share his terrors.

And the days will pass with baffled faces,
then the weeks, then the months,
then there will be a day when no question is asked,
and the knots of grief will loosen in the stomach,
and the puffed faces will calm.
And on that day he will not have ceased,
        but will have ceased to be separated by death.
How long does a man live, after all?

A man lives so many different lengths of time.

Brian Patten

He has outsoared the shadow of our night;
Envy and calumny and hate and pain,
And that unrest which men miscall delight,
Can touch him not and torture not again;
From the contagion of the world's slow stain
He is secure, and now can never mourn
A heart grown cold, a head grown gray in vain...

He is made one with Nature: there is heard
His voice in all her music, from the moan
Of thunder, to the song of night's sweet bird;
He is a presence to be felt and known
In darkness and in light...

He is a portion of the loveliness
Which once he made more lovely...

P.B. Shelley – from Adonais

Some people are bound to die young.
By dying young a person stays young for ever in
people's memory.
If he burns brightly before he dies his light shines
for all time.

Alexander Solzhenitsyn

Doomed to know not Winter, only Spring – a being
Trod the flowery April blithely for a while;
Took his fill of music, joy of thought and seeing,
Came and stayed and went; nor ever ceased to smile.

Came and stayed and went; and now, when all is finished,
You alone have crossed the melancholy stream.
Yours the pang; but his, oh his, the undiminished
Undecaying gladness, undeparted dream.

Robert Louis Stevenson

SUICIDE

It is quite obvious that there is nothing in the world to which every man has a more unassailable title than to his own life and person.

Arthur Schopenhauer – *On Suicide*

THE WORLD'S A STAGE

The world's a stage. The trifling entrance fee
Is paid (by proxy) to the registrar.
The Orchestra is very loud and free
But plays no music in particular.
They do not print a programme, that I know.
The cast is large. There isn't any plot.
The acting of the piece is far below
The very worst of modernistic rot.

The only part about it I enjoy
Is what was called in English the Foyay.
There I will stand awhile and toy
With thought, and set my cigarette alight;
And then – without returning to the play –
On with my coat and out into the night.

Hilaire Belloc

There is but one truly serious philosophical problem and that is suicide. Judging whether life is or is not worth living amounts to answering the fundamental question of philosophy. All the rest – whether or not the world has three dimensions, whether the mind has nine or twelve categories – comes afterwards. ...

Suicide has never been dealt with except as a social phenomenon. On the contrary, we are concerned here, at the outset, with the relationship between individual thought and suicide. An act like this is prepared within the silence of the heart, as is a great work of art. The man is ignorant of it. ...

... Beginning to think is beginning to be undermined. Society has but little connection with such beginnings. The worm is in the man's heart. That is where it must be sought. One must follow and understand the fatal game that leads from lucidity in the face of existence to flight from light.

Albert Camus – from *The Myth of Sisyphus &*
Other Essays

If the room is smoky, if only moderately, I will stay; if there is too much smoke, I will go. Remember this, keep it firmly in mind, the door is always open.

Epictetus

If I can choose between a death of torture and one that is simple and easy, why should I not select the latter? As I choose the ship in which I sail and the house which I inhabit, so I will choose the death by which I leave life.

Lucius Annaeus Seneca

QUATRAINS FROM THE RUBAIYAT
OF OMAR KHAYYAM

The Worldly Hope men set their Hearts upon
Turns Ashes – or it prospers; and anon,
Like Snow upon the Desert's dusty Face
Lighting a little Hour or two – is gone.

... 'Tis all a Chequer-board of Nights and Days
Where Destiny with Men for Pieces plays:
Hither and thither moves, and mates, and slays.
And one by one back in the Closet lays.

... The moving Finger writes; and, having writ,
Moves on; nor all thy Piety nor Wit
Shall lure it back to cancel half a Line,
Nor all thy Tears wash out a word of it.

And that inverted Bowl we call The Sky,
Whereunder crawling coopt we live and die,
Lift not thy hands to *It* for help – for It
Rolls impotently on as Thou or I.

... Alas, that Spring should vanish with the Rose!
That Youth's sweet-scented Manuscript should close!
The Nightingale that in the Branches sang,
Ah, whence, and whither flown again, who knows!

Ah Love! Could thou and I with Fate conspire
To grasp this sorry Scheme of Things entire,
Would not we shatter it to bits – and then
Remould it nearer to the Heart's Desire!

Edward Fitzgerald's translation (1859)

THE ROAD NOT TAKEN

Two roads diverged in a yellow wood,
And sorry I could not travel both
And be one traveller, long I stood
And looked down one as far as I could
To where it bent in undergrowth;

Then took the other, as just as fair,
And having perhaps the better claim,
Because it was grassy and wanted wear;
Though as for that the passing there
Had worn them really about the same,

And both that morning equally lay
In leaves no step had trodden black.
Oh, I kept the first for another day!
Yet knowing how way leads on to way,
I doubted if I should ever come back.

I shall be telling this with a sigh
Somewhere ages and ages hence:
Two roads diverged in a wood, and I –
I took the one less travelled by,
And that has made all the difference.

Robert Frost

HEAVEN-HAVEN

I have desired to go
Where springs not fail,
To fields where flies no sharp and sided hail
And a few lilies blow.

And I have asked to be
Where no storm come,
Where the green swell is in the havens dumb,
And out of the swing of the sea.

Gerard Manley Hopkins

Each and every one of us stands in a peculiar and unique
relationship to his or her life. Our life is our own in the
way in which nothing else is. We could characterize this
relationship by calling it, perhaps somewhat
tendentiously, nontransferable ownership. But we do
own it: that is the major point. And as with anything we
own in the full-blooded sense of that term, we have the
right to advance it, to ruin it, or even to dispose of it
altogether. In short, we have the right to end it if we so
please, to commit suicide... Suicide, therefore, is our
right simply in virtue of a much more general right: the
right to do with our own property as we please.

Eike-Henner Kluge

THE DOUBLE AUTUMN

Better to close the book and say goodnight
When nothing moves you much but your own plight.
Neither the owl's noise through the dying grove
Where the small creatures insecurely move.
Nor what the moon does to the huddled trees,
Nor the admission that such things as these
Would have excited once can now excite.
Better close down the double autumn night
Than practise dumbly staring at your plight.

James Reeves

WHY DO I ...

Why do I think of death as a friend?
It is because he is a scatterer
He scatters the human frame
The nerviness and the great pain
Throws it on the fresh fresh air
And now it is nowhere
Only sweet death does this
Sweet death, kind death,
Of all the gods you are best.

Stevie Smith

COMMITTAL POEMS

But now the journey is over.
Too short, alas, too short.
It was filled with adventure and wisdom,
    laughter and love,
Gallantry and grace.
So farewell, farewell.

> Constantine P. Cavafy

I came unknowing what the light would show;
Found joy, disasters, wonders, guilt and pain;
And cheerfully, unconned by myth, will go
Back to the real, indifferent dark again.

> Harry Bell

CLOUDS

Down the blue night the unending columns press
In noiseless tumult, break and wave and flow,
Now tread the far South, or lift rounds of snow
Up to the white moon's hidden loveliness.
Some pause in their grave wandering comradeless,
And turn with profound gesture vague and slow,
As who would pray good for the world, but know
Their benediction empty as they bless.

They say that the Dead die not, but remain
Near to the rich heirs of their grief and mirth.
I think they ride the calm mid-heaven, as these,
In wise majestic melancholy train,
And watch the moon, and the still-raging seas,
And men, coming and going on the earth.

Rupert Brooke

I fall asleep in the full and certain hope
That my slumber shall not be broken;
And that though I be all-forgetting,
Yet shall I not be all-forgotten,
But continue that life in the thoughts and deeds
Of those I loved...

Samuel Butler

TURN AGAIN TO LIFE

If I should die and leave you here awhile,

Be not like others, sore undone, who keep

Long vigils by silent dust, and weep.

For my sake, turn again to life and smile,

Nerving thy heart and trembling hand to do

Something to comfort weaker hearts than thine.

Complete these dear unfinished tasks of mine

And I perchance may therein comfort you!

Mary Lee Hall

PARTA QUIES

Good-night; ensured release
Imperishable peace,
    Have these for yours,
    While sea abides, and land,
And earth's foundations stand,
    And heaven endures.

When earth's foundations flee,
Nor sky nor land nor sea
    At all is found,
Content you, let them burn:
It is not your concern;
    Sleep on, sleep sound.

A.E. Housman

When I am dead
Cry for me a little
Think of me sometimes
But not too much.
Think of me now and again
As I was in life
At some moments it's pleasant to recall
But not for long.
Leave me in peace
And I shall leave you in peace
And while you live
Let your thoughts be with the living.

Traditional Indian prayer

I strove with none, for none was worth my strife.
Nature I loved and, next to Nature, Art:
I warmed both hands before the fire of life;
It sinks, and I am ready to depart.

Death stands above me, whispering low
I know not what into my ear:
Of his strange language all I know
Is, there is not a word of fear.

Walter Savage Landor

Some would go down by the sunlit sea
And some by the mountain peak,
If they had a choice of where they'd be
When death has paled the cheek;
And some in a sheltered, crowded place
Where the harps of angels play –
But I would go out with the winds that race
Away, away, away!

Will Lawson – from *Unfettered*

EVERYONE SANG

Everyone suddenly burst out singing;
And I was filled with such delight
As prisoned birds must find in freedom,
Winging wildly across the white
Orchards and dark green fields; on – on – and
      out of sight.

Everyone's voice was suddenly lifted;
And beauty came like the setting sun:
My heart was shaken with tears; and horror
Drifted away... O, but Everyone
Was a bird; and the song was wordless; the singing
      will never be done.

Siegfried Sasson

... His life was gentle, and the elements
So mix'd in him, that Nature might stand up,
And say to all the world, 'This was a man!'

William Shakespeare – from *Julius Caesar*

Take me to some high place of heather, rock and ling,
Scatter my dust and ashes, feed me to the wind,
So that I will be part of the curlew's cry and the soaring
   hawk,
The blue milkwort and the sundew hung with diamonds;
I'll be riding the gentle wind that blows through your
   hair,
Reminding you how we shared in the joy of living.

> Ewan MacColl – from the song
> 'The Joy of Living'

Our revels are now ended. These our actors,

As I foretold you, were all spirits and

Melted into air, into thin air:

And, like the baseless fabric of this vision,

The cloud-capp'd towers, the gorgeous palaces,

The solemn temples, the great globe itself,

Yea, all which it inherit, shall dissolve

And, like this insubstantial pageant faded,

Leave not a rack behind. We are such stuff

As dreams are made on, and our little life

Is rounded with a sleep.

> William Shakespeare – from *The Tempest*

What though the radiance which was once so bright
Be now for ever taken from my sight,
  Though nothing can bring back the hour
Of splendour in the grass, of glory in the flower;
    We will grieve not, rather find
    Strength in what remains behind.

> William Wordsworth – from *Intimations of Immortality*

And when the stream that overflows has passed,
A consciousness remains upon the silent shore of
    memory;
Images and precious thoughts that shall not be
And cannot be destroyed.

> William Wordsworth – from *The Excursion*

ENVOIS

They are not long, the weeping and the laughter,
　Love and desire and hate;
I think they have no portion in us after
We pass the gate.

They are not long, the days of wine and roses;
　Out of a misty dream
Our path emerges for a while, then closes
　Within a dream.

　　　　Ernest Dowson

I have got my leave. Bid me farewell, my brothers!
I bow to you all and take my departure.
Here I give back the keys of my door – and I give up all
  claims to my house.
I only ask for last kind words from you.

We were neighbours for long, but I received more than
  I could give.
Now the day has dawned and the lamp that lit my dark
  corner is out.
A summons has come and I am ready for my journey.

Rabindranath Tagore – from *Gitanjali XCIII*

ON MIDDLETON EDGE

If this life-saving rock should fail
Yielding too much to my embrace,
And rock and I to death should race
The rock would stay there in the dale.
While I, breaking my fall
Would still go on
Further than any wandering star has gone.

Andrew Young

LAST LINES FOR A MATERIALIST

Give me no grave, who loved the summer sky;
  Not dark decay but purifying flame.
And set no stone to grieve the passer-by;
  Let thought and substance vanish, whence they came,
Into the elements that build the star,
  The breath of life and busy mind of man –
So shall my dust discover what we are
  And win its deepest peace since Time began.
If epitaph you seek, write this on air,
  "He loved the green earth and his fellow men;
Nature and Cause were his especial care;
  He touched the hem of Truth and, now and then,
Testing old faiths he said, with proffered hand,
  'You would believe, but I must understand'."

Anon

FAREWELL

Farewell to Thee! But not farewell
To all my fondest thoughts of Thee;
Within my heart they still shall dwell
And they shall cheer and comfort me.

Life seems more sweet that Thou didst live
And men more true that Thou wert one;
Nothing is lost that Thou didst give,
Nothing destroyed that Thou hast done.

Anne Brontë

... But pleasures are like poppies spread –
You seize the flow'r, its bloom is shed;
Or like the snow falls in the river –
A moment white, then melts for ever;
Or like the borealis race,
That flit ere you can point their place;
Or, like the rainbow's lovely form
Evanishing amid the storm...

Robert Burns – from '*Tam O'Shanter*'

He has completed his voyage; he has gone beyond
  sorrow.
The fetters of life have fallen from him and he lives in
  full freedom.
The thoughtful strive always; they have no fixed abode,
  but leave home like swans from their lake.
Like the flight of birds in the sky, it is hard to follow the
  path of the selfless.
They have no possessions, but live on alms in a world of
  freedom.
Like the flight of birds in the sky, it is hard to follow
  their path.
With their senses under control, temperate in eating, they
  know the meaning of freedom.
Even the gods envy the saints, whose senses obey them
  like well-trained horses and who are free from pride.
Patient like the earth they stand like a threshold.
They are pure like a lake without mud and free from the
cycle of birth and death.
Wisdom has stilled their minds and their thoughts, words
and deeds are filled with peace.

Freed from illusion, and from personal ties, they have
renounced the world of appearance to find reality.
Thus they have reached the highest.
They make holy wherever they dwell, in village or forest,
   on land or at sea.
With their senses at peace, and their minds full of joy,
they make the forests holy.

> Verses translated from the Buddhist scriptures
> (*Dhammapada*)

That such have died enables us
The tranquiller to die:
That such have lived certificate
For immortality.

> Emily Dickinson

WHAT IS SUCCESS?

To laugh often and love much, to win the respect of intelligent persons and the affection of children; to earn the approbation of honest critics and to endure the betrayal of false friends; to appreciate beauty; to find the best in others; to give one's self; to leave the world a bit better, whether by a healthy child, a garden patch or a redeemed social condition; to have played and laughed with enthusiasm and sung with exultation; to know even one life has breathed easier because you have lived, this is to have succeeded.

Ralph Waldo Emerson

If I should go before the rest of you,
Break not a flower, nor inscribe a stone,
Nor, when I'm gone, speak in a Sunday voice,
But be the usual selves that I have known.
Weep if you must,
Parting is hell,
But life goes on,
So sing as well.

Joyce Grenfell – from *Joyce by Herself and Her Friends*

FAREWELL

Farewell dear friends
I loved you so much
But now I must leave you
And spread over me the dust

Fair life fare well
Fare never ill
Far I go now
And say, Farewell.

Farewell dear world
With the waters around you curled
And the grass on your breast
I loved you best.

Farewell fish and insect
Bird, animal, swift mover
Grim reptile as well
I was your approver.

Wide sky, farewell,
Sun, moon, stars in places
Farewell all fair universes
In far places.

Stevie Smith

FAREWELL MY FRIENDS

It was beautiful
As long as it lasted
The journey of my life.

I have no regrets
Whatsoever save
The pain I'll leave behind.
Those dear hearts
Who love and care...
And the strings pulling
At the heart and soul...

The strong arms
That held me up
When my own strength
Let me down.

At every turning of my life
I came across
Good friends,
Friends who stood by me
Even when the time raced me by.

Farewell, farewell
My friends
I smile and
Bid you goodbye.
No, shed no tears
For I need them not
All I need is your smile.

If you feel sad
Do think of me
For that's what I'll like.
When you live in the hearts
Of those you love
Remember then
You never die.

Rabindranath Tagore

AND DEATH SHALL HAVE NO DOMINION

And death shall have no dominion.
Dead men naked they shall be one
With the man in the wind and the west moon;
When their bones are picked clean
   and the clean bones gone,
They shall have stars at elbow and foot;
Though they go mad they shall be sane,
Though they sink through the sea
   they shall rise again;
Though lovers be lost love shall not;
And death shall have no dominion.

And death shall have no dominion.
Under the windings of the sea
They lying long shall not die windily;
Twisting on racks when sinews give way,
Strapped to a wheel, yet shall not break;
Faith in their hands shall snap in two,
And the unicorn evils run them through;
Split all ends up they shan't crack;
And death shall have no dominion.

And death shall have no dominion.
No more may gulls cry at their ears
Or waves break loud on the seashores;
Where blew a flower may a flower no more
Lift its head to the blows of the rain;
Though they be mad and dead as nails,
Heads of the characters hammer through daises;
Break in the sun till the sun breaks down,
And death shall have no dominion.

> Dylan Thomas

TO A DESCENDANT

I shall not be an importunate, nagging ghost,
Sighing for unsaid prayers: or a family spectre
Advertising that someone is due to join me...
Nor one who has to be exorcised by the Rector.

I shall not be the commercial type of ghost,
Pointing to boxes of gold under the floor
And I certainly don't intend to jangle chains
Or carry my head... (such a gruesome type of chore!)

I shall not cause draughts, be noisy, spoil your 'let', –
In fact, to be brief, I shan't materialise.
But I shall be pleased if anyone ever sees me
In your face or your walk or the glance of your
     laughing eyes.

Lorna Wood

WEDDINGS

THE OCCASION AND
ITS INTENTIONS

LOVE POEMS – PAST

LOVE POEMS – PRESENT

THE ART OF MARRIAGE

COMMENDATIONS

THE OCCASION AND ITS INTENTIONS

Look to this day
for it is life
the very life of life.
In its brief course lie all
the realities and truths
of existence,
the joy of growth,
the splendour of action,
the glory of power.
For yesterday is
but a memory.
And tomorrow is
only a vision.
But today well lived
makes every yesterday
a memory of happiness
and every tomorrow
a vision of hope.
Look well, therefore,
to this day.

> – from the ancient Sanskrit

EPITHALAMION

Singing, today I married my white girl
beautiful in a barley field.
Green on thy finger a grass blade curled,
so, with this ring I thee wed, I thee wed,
and send our love to the loveless world
of all the living and all the dead.

Now, no more than vulnerable human,
we, more than one, less than two,
are nearly ourselves in a barley field –
and only love is the rent that's due
though the bailiffs of time return anew
to all the living but not the dead.

Shipwrecked, the sun sinks down harbours
of a sky, unloads its liquid cargoes
of marigolds, and I and my white girl
lie still in the barley – who else wishes
to speak, what more can be said
by all the living against all the dead?

Come then all you wedding guests:
green ghost of trees, gold of barley,
you blackbird priests in the field,
you wind that shakes the pansy head
fluttering on a stalk like a butterfly;
come the living and come the dead.

Listen flowers, birds, winds, worlds,
tell all today that I have married
more than a white girl in the barley –
for today I took to my human bed
flower and bird and wind and world,
and all the living and all the dead.

Dannie Abse

RAIN SOMETIMES

Rain sometimes,
Money down the drain sometimes,
Reason to complain sometimes,
That's how it will be;
But there'll be champagne sometimes,
Lobster flown from Maine sometimes,
We'll ride the gravy-train sometimes,
Just you wait and see.

We may be stranded in the rain sometimes,
Dream our dreams in vain sometimes,
Lose more than we gain sometimes,
But this I guarantee:
Love is not for sometimes,
Love is for all times,
For all times,
For you and me.

> Popular Song – music and lyrics by Arthur Hamilton

TRUE WAYS OF KNOWING

Not an ounce excessive, not an inch too little,
Our easy reciprocations. You let me know
The way a boat would feel, if it could feel,
The intimate support of water.

The news you bring me has been news forever,
So that I understand what a stone would say
If only a stone could speak. Is it sad a grassblade
Can't know how it is lovely?

Is it sad that you can't know, except by hearsay
(My gossiping failing words) that you are the way
A water is that can clench its palm and crumple
A boat's confiding timbers?

But that's excessive, and too little. Knowing
The way a circle would describe its roundness,
We touch two selves and feel, complete and gentle,
The intimate support of being.

The way that flight would feel a bird flying
(if it could feel) is the way a space that's in
A stone that's in a water would know itself
If it had our way of knowing.

Norman MacCaig

GATHERING

Here, in our best bib and tucker we flock,
drawn from all the hell over, iron filings to love's
    magnet,
an intricate pattern, a one-time convergence
of friends and relations, a living mandala;

young and old, nephews and nieces,
sisters, brothers, parents, grandfather,
and all those others you got to choose for yourselves,
agglomerating to hold you in the center.

Slow in coming, swift in passing, this day,
slow but long-lasting the major choice confirmed,
hardly inevitable, yet falling into place
as though it were just what we always expected.

So, * * * * * * and * * * * * *, we join as you join
in celebrating love – yours for each other, of course,
ours, as you must know, for you – circling,
cherishing, blessing, releasing,
love, the core of it all.

                William H. Matchett

SOMETIMES

Sometimes things don't go, after all,
from bad to worse. Some years, muscatel
faces down frost; green thrives; the crops don't fail
sometimes a man aims high, and all goes well.

A people sometimes will step back from war;
elect an honest man; decide they care
enough, that they can't leave some stranger poor.
Some men become what they were born for.

Sometimes our best efforts do not go
amiss; sometimes we do as we meant to.
The sun will sometimes melt a field of sorrow
that seemed hard frozen: may it happen for you.

Sheenagh Pugh

TODAY

Today I marry my friend,
The one I have laughed and cried with,
The one I have learned from and shared with,
The one I have chosen to support, encourage,
And give myself to, through all the days
Given us to share.
Today I marry the one I love.

Bertrand Russell

FOR AN UNBORN BABY

If she's a girl,
I hope she'll stretch her wings
and grow up free, wide ranging
like a seagull, dealing with the winds
competently, swifting on currents of air,
able to live on anything she can find
in the murky sea, or even on rubbish heaps,
adapting with ease when storms drive her inland.
May she choose wisely if in the end
she settles on one name, one piece of ground.

May she banish those who'd seek to protect her
from heartbreak, or joy.
– And may he achieve no less
if he's a boy.

Janet Shepperson

HE WISHES FOR THE CLOTHS
OF HEAVEN

Had I the heavens' embroidered cloths,
Enwrought with golden and silver light,
The blue and the dim and the dark cloths
Of night and light and the half-light,
I would spread the cloths under your feet:
But I, being poor, have only my dreams;
I have spread my dreams under your feet;
Tread softly, because you tread on my dreams.

W.B. Yeats

You are part of me. I do not know
By what slow chemistry you first became
A vital fibre of my being. Go
Beyond the rim of time or space, the same
Inflections of your voice will sing their way
Into the depths of my mind still. Your hair
Will gleam as bright, the artless play
Of word and glance, gesture and the fair
Young fingers waving, have too deeply etched
The pattern of your soul on mine. Forget
Me quickly as a laughing picture sketched
On water, I shall never know regret
Knowing no magic ever can set free
That part of you that is a part of me.

   Frank Yerby

LOVE POEMS - PAST

THE CONFIRMATION

Yes, yours, my love, is the right human face.
I in my mind had waited for this long,
Seeing the false and searching for the true,
Then found you as a traveller finds a place
Of welcome suddenly amid the wrong
Valleys and rocks and twisting roads. But you,
What shall I call you? A fountain in a waste,
A well of water in a country dry,
Or anything that's honest and good, an eye
That makes the whole world bright. Your open heart,
Simple with giving, gives the primal deed,
The first good world, the blossom, the blowing seed,
The hearth, the steadfast land, the wandering sea,
Not beautiful or rare in every part,
But like yourself, as they were meant to be.

Edwin Muir

How do I love thee? Let me count the ways.
   I love thee to the depth and breadth and height
   My soul can reach, when feeling out of sight
For the ends of Being and ideal Grace.
I love thee to the level of every day's
   Most quiet need, by sun and candle-light.
   I love thee freely, as men strive for right;
I love thee purely, as they turn from praise.
I love thee with the passion put to use
   In my old griefs, and with my childhood's faith.
I love thee with a love I seemed to lose
   With my lost saints – I love thee with the breath,
Smiles, tears, of all my life! – and, if God choose,
   I shall but love thee better after death.

Eliabeth Barrett Browning from Sonnets from the Portuguese

NOW

Out of your whole life give but a moment!
All of your life that has gone before,
All to come after it – so you ignore,
So you make perfect the present, – condense,
In a rapture of rage, for perfection's endowment,
Thought and feeling and soul and sense –
Merged in a moment which gives me at last
You around me for once, you beneath me, above me, –
Me – sure that despite of time future, time past, –
This tick of our life-time's one moment you love me!
How long such suspension may linger? Ah sweet –
The moment eternal – just that and no more –
When ecstasy's utmost we clutch at the core
While cheeks burn, arms open, eyes shut and lips meet!

Robert Browning

THE GOOD-MORROW

I wonder by my troth, what thou and I
Did, till we lov'd? were we not wean'd till then?
But suck'd on countrey pleasures childishly?
Or snorted we i'the seaven sleepers den?
'Twas so; But this, all pleasures fancies bee.
If ever any beauty I did see,
Which I desir'd , and got, t'was but a dreame of thee.

And now good morrow to our waking soules,
Which watch not one another out of feare;
For love, all love of other sights controules,
And makes one little roome, an every where.
Let sea-discoverers to new worlds have gone,
Let Maps to other, worlds on worlds have showne,
Let us possesse one world, each hath one, and is one.

My face in thine eye, thine in mine appeares,
And true plaine hearts doe in the faces rest,
Where can we finde two better hemispheres
Without sharpe North, without declining West?
What ever dyes, was not mixt equally;
If our two loves be one, or, thou and I
Love so alike, that none doe slacken, none can die.

John Donne

SO WHAT IS LOVE?

So what is Love? If thou wouldst know
The heart alone can tell:
Two minds with but a single thought,
Two hearts that beat as one.

And whence comes Love? Like morning bright
Love comes without thy call.
And how dies Love? A spirit bright,
Love never dies at all.

Anonymous – translated by Maria Lovell

LOVE IS NOT ALL

Love is not all: it is not meat nor drink
Nor slumber nor a roof against the rain;
Nor yet a floating spar to men that sink
And rise and sink and rise and sink again;
Love cannot fill the thickened lung with breath,
Nor clean the blood, nor set the fractured bone;
Yet many a man is making friends with death
Even as I speak, for lack of love alone.
It well may be that in a difficult hour,
Pinned down by pain and moaning for release,
Or nagged by want past resolution's power,
I might be driven to sell your love for peace,
Or trade the memory of this night for food.
It well may be. I do not think I would.

Edna St Vincent Millay

SONNET

I wish I could remember that first day,
First hour, first moment of your meeting me,
If bright or dim the season, it might be
Summer or Winter for aught I can say;
So unrecorded did it slip away,
So blind was I to see and forsee,
So dull to mark the budding of my tree
That would not blossom yet for many a May.
If only I could recollect it, such
A day of days! I let it come and go
As traceless as a thaw of byegone snow;
It seemed to mean so little, meant so much;
If only now I could recall that touch,
First touch of hand in hand – Did one but know!

Christina Rossetti

SONNET 116

Let me not to the marriage of true minds
Admit impediments. Love is not love
Which alters when it alteration finds,
Or bends with the remover to remove:
O, no! – it is an ever-fixed mark
That looks on tempests and is never shaken;
It is the star to every wand'ring barque,
Whose worth's unknown although his height be taken.
Love's not time's fool, though rosy lips and cheeks
Within his bending sickle's compass come;
Love alters not with his brief hours and weeks,
But bears it out even to the edge of doom.
    If this be error and upon me proved,
    I never writ, nor no man ever loved.

William Shakespeare

TO_____

One word is too often profaned
   For me to profane it,
One feeling too falsely disdained
   For thee to disdain it;
One hope is too like despair
   For prudence to smother,
And pity from thee more dear
   Than that from another.

I can give not what men call love,
   But wilt thou accept not
The worship the heart lifts above
   And the Heavens reject not, –
The desire of the moth for the star,
   Of the night for the morrow,
The devotion to something afar
   From the sphere of our sorrow?

      P.B. Shelley

THE BARGAIN

My true love hath my heart, and I have his,
　By just exchange, one for the other given.
I hold his dear, and mine he cannot miss,
　There never was a better bargain driven.
His heart in me keeps me and him in one,
　My love in him his thoughts and senses guides;
He loves my heart, for once it was his own,
　I cherish his, because in me it bides.
His heart his wound received from my sight,
　My heart was wounded with his wounded heart;
For as from me on him his hurt did light,
　So still me thought in me his hurt did smart.
Both equal hurt, in this change sought our bliss:
My true love hath my heart and I have his.

Sir Philip Sidney

NO, NO, FAIR HERETIC

No, no, fair heretic, it needs must be
    But an ill love in me,
    And worse for thee.

For were it in my power,
To love thee now this hour
    More than I did the last:

I would then so fall,
    I might not love at all.

Love that can flow, and can admit increase,
Admits as well an ebb, and may grow less.

True love is still the same; the torrid zones,
    And those more frigid ones,
    It must not know.
For love, grown cold or hot,
    Is lust or friendship, not
    The thing we have.

For that's a flame would die,
Held down or up too high:

    Then think I love more than I can express,
    And would love more, could I but love thee less.

        Sir John Suckling

It is for the union of you and me
that there is light in the sky.
It is for the union of you and me
that the earth is decked in dusky green.
It is for the union of you and me
that night sits motionless with the world in her arms;
dawn appears opening the eastern door
with sweet murmurs in her voice.

The boat of hope sails along on the currents of
eternity towards that union,
flowers of the ages are being gathered together
for its welcoming ritual.

It is for the union of you and me
that this heart of mine, in the garb of a bride,
has proceeded from birth to birth
upon the surface of this ever-turning world
to choose the beloved.

Rabindranath Tagore

THE OWL AND THE PUSSYCAT

The owl and the pussycat went to sea
In a beautiful pea-green boat.
They took some honey and plenty of money,
Wrapped up in a five-pound note.
The owl looked up to the stars above
And sang to a small guitar:
'Oh, lovely pussy, oh pussy my love,
What a beautiful pussy you are, you are;
What a beautiful pussy you are.'

Pussy said to the owl, 'You elegant fowl,
How charmingly sweet you sing.
Oh, let us be married, too long we have tarried,
But what shall we do for a ring?'
So they sailed away for a year and a day
To the land where the bong tree grows.
And there in a wood a piggy-wig stood
With a ring in the end of his nose, his nose;
With a ring in the end of his nose.

'Dear pig, are you willing to sell for one shilling
Your ring?' Said the piggy: 'I will.'
So they sailed away and were married next day

By the turkey who lives on the hill.
They dined on mince and slices of quince
Which they ate with a runcible spoon.
And hand in hand, on the edge of the sand,
They danced by the light of the moon, the moon;
They danced by the light of the moon.

Edward Lear

LOVE POEMS - PRESENT

I LOVE YOU...

I love you ...
For the kindness in your eyes
   and the warmth in your voice,
For the honesty of your words
   and the silence of your smile;
For the ways in which we're similar,
   and those in which we're worlds apart.
For the openness of your understanding
   and the acceptance of your heart;
For the tenderness of your touch
   and the strength of your commitment,
For your sense of humour
   and your seriousness of purpose;
For a thousand small reasons,
   and one most important of all:
Simply because you are you.
In all of creation you are the one whom I cherish most,
The one with whom I hope to share my life –
Its joys, its sorrows, its accomplishments, its challenges –
While building our dreams together and growing every
   day
In the love that makes us one.

              Anon

OH TELL ME THE TRUTH
ABOUT LOVE

Some say that love's a little boy,
    And some say it's a bird,
Some say it makes the world go round,
    And some say that's absurd,
And when I asked the man next-door,
    Who looked as if he knew,
His wife got very cross indeed,
    And said it wouldn't do.

Does it look like a pair of pyjamas,
    Or the ham in a temperance hotel?
Does its odour remind one of llamas,
    Or has it a comforting smell?
Is it prickly to touch as a hedge is,
    Or soft as eiderdown fluff?
Is it sharp or quite smooth at the edges?
    O tell me the truth about love.

Our history books refer to it
    In cryptic little notes,
It's quite a common topic on
    The Transatlantic boats;
I've found the subject mentioned in
    Accounts of suicides,
And even seen it scribbled on
    The backs of railway-guides.

Does it howl like a hungry Alsatian,
   Or boom like a military band?
Could one give a first-rate imitation
   On a saw or a Steinway Grand?
Is its singing at parties a riot?
   Does it only like Classical stuff?
Will it stop when one wants to be quiet?
   O tell me the truth about love.

I looked inside the summer-house;
   It wasn't ever there:
I tried the Thames at Maidenhead,
   And Brighton's bracing air.
I don't know what the blackbird sang,
   Or what the tulip said;
But it wasn't in the chicken-run,
   Or underneath the bed.

Can it pull extraordinary faces?
   Is it usually sick on a swing?
Does it spend all its time at the races,
   Or fiddling with pieces of string?
Has it views of its own about money?
   Does it think Patriotism enough?
Are its stories vulgar but funny?
   O tell me the truth about love.

When it comes, will it come without warning
    Just as I'm picking my nose?
Will it knock on my door in the morning,
    Or tread in the bus on my toes?
Will it come like a change in the weather?
    Will its greeting be courteous or rough?
Will it alter my life altogether?
    O tell me the truth about love.

           W. H. Auden XII – Twelve Songs

THE ORANGE

At lunchtime I bought a huge orange –
The size of it made us all laugh.
I peeled it and shared it with Robert and Dave –
They got quarters and I had a half.

And that orange, it made me so happy,
As ordinary things often do
Just lately. The shopping. A walk in the park.
This is peace and contentment. It's new.

The rest of the day was quite easy.
I did all the jobs on my list
And enjoyed them and had some time over.
I love you. I'm glad I exist.

           Wendy Cope

THIS IS TO LET YOU KNOW

This is to let you know
That there was no moon last night
And that the tide was high
And that on the broken horizon glimmered the lights
   of ships
Twenty at least, like a sedate procession passing by.

This is to let you know
That when I'd turned out the lamp
And in the dark I lay
That suddenly piercing loneliness, like a knife,
Twisted my heart, for you were such a long long
   way away.

This is to let you know
That there are no English words
That ever could explain
How, quite without warning, lovingly you were here
Holding me close, smoothing away the idiotic pain.

This is to let you know
That all that I feel for you
Can never wholly go.
I love you and miss you, even two hours away,
With all my heart. This is to let you know.

              Noel Coward

LOVES COMES QUIETLY

Love comes quietly,
finally drops
about me, on me,
in the old ways.

What did I know
thinking myself
able to go
alone all the way.

Robert Creeley

I CARRY YOUR HEART WITH ME

i carry your heart with me(i carry it in
my heart)i am never without it(anywhere
i go you go,my dear;and whatever is done
by only me is your doing,my darling)
                            i fear
no fate(for you are my fate,my sweet)i want
no world(for beautiful you are my world,my true)
and it's you are whatever a moon has always meant
and whatever a sun will always sing is you

here is the deepest secret nobody knows
(here is the root of the root and the bud of the bud
and the sky of the sky of a tree called life;which grows
higher than soul can hope or mind can hide)
and this is the wonder that's keeping the stars apart

i carry your heart(i carry it in my heart)

                E. E. Cummings

VALENTINE

Not a red rose or a satin heart.

I give you an onion.
It is a moon wrapped in brown paper.
It promises light
like the careful undressing of love.

Here.
It will blind you with tears
like a lover.
It will make your reflection
a wobbling photo of grief.

I am trying to be truthful.

Not a cute card or a kissogram.

I give you an onion.
Its fierce kiss will stay on your lips,
possessive and faithful
as we are,
for as long as we are.

Take it.
Its platinum loops shrink to a wedding ring,
if you like.
Lethal.
Its scent will cling to your fingers,
cling to your knife.

Carol Ann Duffy

BY LOCH ETIVE

The flowers of the flags
Are like yellow birds, hanging
Over the secret pool.

The fronds of the ferns
Are like green serpents, curling
Beside the silent path.

The lashes of your lids
Are like a bird's wing sweeping
Across your regard.

The softness of your speech
Is like rain, falling
Among parched thoughts.

The lenience of your lips
Is like a cloud dissolving
At the kiss of the wind.

From your deep consideration
Runs the dark stream, nourishing
The lake of my delight.

Bryan Guinness

LOVE POEM

There is a shyness that we have
Only with those whom we most love.
Something it has to do also
With how we cannot bring to mind
A face whose every line we know.
O love is kind, O love is kind.

That there should still remain the first
Sweetness, also the later thirst –
This is why pain must play some part
In all true feelings that we find
And every shaking of the heart.
O love is kind, O love is kind.

And it is right that we should want
Discretion, secrecy, no hint
Of what we share. Love which cries out,
And wants the world to understand,
Is love that holds itself in doubt.
For love is quiet, and love is kind.

Elizabeth Jennings

THE SUN HAS BURST THE SKY

The sun has burst the sky
Because I love you
And the river its banks.

The sea laps the great rocks
Because I love you
And takes no heed of the moon dragging it away
And saying coldly 'Constancy is not for you'.

The blackbird fills the air
Because I love you
With spring and lawns and shadows falling on lawns.

The people walk in the street and laugh
I love you
And far down the river ships sound their hooters
Crazy with joy because I love you.

Jenny Joseph

STRAWBERRIES

There were never strawberries
like the ones we had
that sultry afternoon
Sitting on the step
of the open french window
facing each other
your knees held in mine
the blue plates in our laps
the strawberries glistening
in the hot sunlight
we dipped them in sugar
looking at each other
not hurrying the feast
for one to come
the empty plates
laid on the stone together
with the two forks crossed
and I bent towards you
sweet in that air
in my arms
abandoned like a child
from your eager mouth
the taste of strawberries in my memory
lean back again
let me love you

let the sun beat
on our forgetfulness
one hour of all
the heat intense
and summer lightning
on the Kilpatrick hills
let the storm wash the plates

Edwin Morgan

THE DIFFERENCE

We watch the gathering sea through sepia dusk
Across a beach of fish-heads, glass beads, relics
Dumped by a careless deity called chance.
Ferry and trawler exchange a passing glance.

Dark comes fast: lighthouse and streetlamp pierce it.
You sit at the window, silent as I write.
We are no longer locked in self-defence.
Being with you has made all the difference.

Neil Powell

NOTES ON LOVE AND COURAGE
the quiet thoughts
of two people a long time in love
touch lightly
like birds nesting in each other's warmth
you will know them by their laughter
but to each other
they speak mostly through their solitude
if they find themselves apart
they may dream of sitting undisturbed
in each other's presence
of wrapping themselves warmly
in each other's ease

Hugh Prather

STARS MAY FALL IN ONE'S HAND

When you are with me, I, who am all too sane, am a little mad.

Through you I see colours where yesterday were grey, black, white, and tomorrow perhaps grey, black, white will be again.

Your eyes reflect impossible towns, trees, flowers, inconceivable lights and faces.

Your voice holds incredible echoes of unlikely words.

Your time has no days, hours, minutes;

And all things are possible;

And stars, like snow, may fall in one's hand.

A.S.J. Tessimond

... Love one another, but make not a bond of love:
Let it rather be a moving sea between the shores
   of your souls.
Fill each other's cup but drink not from one cup.
Give one another of your bread but not from
   the same loaf.
Sing and dance together and be joyous, but let each of
you be alone.
Even as the strings of a lute are alone though they quiver
with the same music.
Give your hearts, but not into each other's keeping.
For only the hand of Life can contain your hearts.
And stand together yet not too near together:
For the pillars of the temple stand apart,
And the oak tree and the cypress grow not in each
other's shadow.

Kahlil Gibran from *The Prophet*

THE ART OF MARRIAGE

To love one another you must try to understand one another, and to understand one another you have to be able to communicate. Whether that communication is done in words or in silent action matters not. As long as it is done in love your heart is open and the love flows freely. Where there is love there can be no language barriers, for love can be conveyed in action, in silent look, in the smallest deed. For love is so great it can be felt or sensed. Your eyes, your heart, your attitude, your whole being can convey what you are feeling towards one another. Just open your heart and let it flow.

Eileen Caddy – from *Footprints On The Path*

LOVE WILL NOT BE CONSTRAINED BY MASTERY

… Love will not be constrained by mastery;
When mastery comes the god of love anon
Stretches his wings and farewell! he is gone.
Love is a thing as any spirit free;
Women by nature long for liberty
And not to be constrained or made a thrall,
And so do men, if I may speak for all.

Whoever's the most patient under love
Has the advantage and will rise above
The other; patience is a conquering virtue.

The learned say that, if it not desert you,
It vanquishes what force can never reach;
Why answer back at every angry speech?
No, learn forbearance or, I'll tell you what,
You will be taught it, whether you will or not.
No one alive – it needs no arguing –
But sometimes says or does a wrongful thing;
Star-constellation, temper, woe or wine
Spur us to wrongful words or make us trip.
One should not seek revenge for every slip,
And temperance from the times must take her schooling
In those that are to learn the art of ruling.

And so this wise and honourable knight
Promised forbearance to her that he might
Live the more easily, and she, as kind,
Promised there never would be fault to find
In her. Thus in this humble, wise accord
She took a servant when she took a lord,
A Lord in marriage in a love renewed
By service, lordship set in servitude;
In servitude? Why no, but far above
Since he had both his lady and his love.
His lady certainly, his wife no less,
To which the law of love will answer 'yes'...

Geoffrey Chaucer (translated Neville Coghill)
– from *The Canterbury Tales* – 'The Franklin's Tale'

It is not enough to love passionately: you must also love well. A passionate love is good doubtless, but a beautiful love is better. May you have as much strength as gentleness; may it lack nothing, not even forbearance, and let even a little compassion be mingled with it... you are human, and because of this capable of much suffering. If then something of compassion does not enter into the feelings you have for one another, these feelings will not always befit all the circumstances of your life together; they will be like festive robes that will not shield you from wind and rain. We love truly only those we love even in their weakness and their poverty. To forbear, to forgive, to console – that alone is the science of love.

Anatole France – from *The Honey Bee*

A successful marriage is one where each partner discovers that it is better to give love than to receive it. To truly love another person is to wish that person to develop and flourish in his or her own terms.

In a long marriage there will be joy and laughter, but also sadness and sorrow, harmony and discord, as you strive to overcome adversity and fulfil your dreams.

The key value of wedlock is that it allows for intimacy between a woman and a man, who can enjoy each other's company, share ideals and expectations, confess failures and admit defeats to each other, and yet realise in union the qualities of the good life.

As you build your home, embark upon careers, and raise a family, your marriage can become a work of art in which both of you together give it line and form, colour and tone. You will be challenged every day and in every way to make your marriage work. If you do, it can become a thing of beauty, a joint creation of aesthetic splendour and enduring value.

Paul Kurtz

ADVICE

To keep your marriage brimming
With love in the loving cup,
Whenever you're wrong, admit it;
Whenever you're right, shut up.

Ogden Nash

When you love someone you do not love them all the
time in exactly the same way, from moment to moment.
It is an impossibility. It is even a lie to pretend to. And
yet this is exactly what most of us demand. We have so
little faith in the ebb and flow of life, of love, of
relationships. We leap at the flow of the tide and resist in
terror its ebb. We are afraid it will never return. We
insist on permanency, on duration, on continuity; when
the only continuity possible in life, as in love, is in
growth, in fluidity – in freedom, in the sense that the
dancers are free, barely touching as they pass, but
partners in the same pattern.

The only real security is not in owning or possessing,
not in demanding or expecting, not in hoping even.
Security in a relationship lies in neither looking back to
what it was in nostalgia, nor forward to what it might be
in dread or anticipation, but living in the present
relationship and accepting it as it is now. For relationships
too, must be like islands, one must accept them for what
they are here and now, within their limits – islands,
surrounded and interrupted by the sea, and continually
visited and abandoned by the tides. One must accept the
security of the winged life, of the ebb and flow, of
intermittency.

Anne Morrow Lindbergh – from Gift from the Sea

MARRIAGE JOINS TWO PEOPLE IN THE CIRCLE OF ITS LOVE

Marriage is a commitment to life, the best that two people can find and bring out in each other. It offers opportunities for sharing and growth that no other relationship can equal. It is a physical and an emotional joining that is promised for a lifetime.

Within the circle of its love, marriage encompasses all of life's most important relationships. A wife and husband are each other's best friend, confidant, lover, teacher, listener and critic. And there may come times when one partner is heartbroken or ailing, and the love of the other may resemble the tender caring of a parent for a child.

Marriage deepens and enriches every facet of life. Happiness is full, memories are fresher, commitment is stronger, even anger is felt more strongly, and passes away more quickly.

Marriage understands and forgives the mistakes life is unable to avoid. It encourages and nurtures new life, new experiences, and new ways of expressing a love that is deeper than life.

When two people pledge their love and care for each other in marriage, they create a spirit unique unto themselves which binds them closer than any spoken or written words. Marriage is a promise, a potential made in the hearts of two people who love each other and takes a lifetime to fulfil.

Edmund O'Neill

THE ART OF A GOOD MARRIAGE

A good marriage must be created.

In the marriage, the little things are the big things...

It is never being too old to hold hands.

It is remembering to say "I love you" at least once each day.

It is never going to sleep angry.

It is having a mutual sense of values and common objectives.

It is standing together and facing the world.

It is forming a circle of love that gathers in the whole family.

It is speaking words of appreciation and demonstrating gratitude in thoughtful ways.

It is having the capacity to forgive and forget.

It is giving each other an atmosphere in which each can grow.

It is a common search for the good and the beautiful.

It is not only marrying the right person, it is being the right partner.

Wilfred Arlan Peterson

We are each a secret to the other. To know one another cannot mean to know everything about each other; it means to feel mutual affection and confidence, and to believe in one another. To analyse others is a rude commencement, for there is a modesty of the soul which we must recognise just as we do that of the body. No one has the right to say to another: "Because we belong to each other as we do, I have a right to know all your thoughts." Not even a mother may treat her child in that way. All demands of this sort are foolish and unwholesome. In this matter giving is the only valuable process; it is only giving that stimulates. Impart as much as you can of your spiritual being to those who are on the road with you, and accept as something precious what comes back to you from them.

> Albert Schweitzer – from *Memoirs of Childhood and Youth*

I WILL MAKE YOU BROOCHES

I will make you brooches and toys for your delight
Of bird-song at morning and star-shine at night.
I will make a palace fit for you and me
Of green days in forests and blue days at sea.

I will make my kitchen, and you shall keep your room,
Where white flows the river and bright blows the broom,
And you shall wash your linen and keep your body white
In rainfall at morning and dewfall at night.

And this shall be for music when no one else is near,
The fine song for singing, the rare song to hear!
That only I remember, that only you admire,
Of the broad road that stretches and the roadside fire.

Robert Louis Stevenson

COMMENDATIONS

The peace of the running water to you,
The peace of the flowing air to you,
The peace of the quiet earth to you,
The peace of the shining stars to you,
And the love and the care of us all to you.

A Celtic Benediction, or 'well-wishing'

'Now you will feel no rain, for each of you will be
shelter for the other;
Now you will feel no cold, for each of you will be
warmth to the other;
Now there is no more loneliness;
Now you are two persons, but there is only one life
before you.
Go now to your dwelling to enter into your life together;
And may your days be good and long upon the earth.'

– from a Native American wedding ceremony

Honour, riches, marriage-blessings,
Long continuance, and increasing,
Hourly joys be still upon you
Juno sings her blessings on you.

Earth's increase, foison plenty,
Barns and garners never empty;
Vines with clustering bunches growing;
Plants with goodly burthen bowing;
Spring come to you at the farthest
In the very end of harvest!
Scarcity and want shall shun you;
Ceres' blessing so is on you.

William Shakespeare – adapted from *The Tempest*

NAMING
CEREMONIES

THE NEW BORN

CHILDREN

THE FUTURE

THE NEW BORN

FROM SPIRALLING
ECSTATICALLY THIS

from spiralling ecstatically this

proud nowhere of earth's most prodigious night
blossoms a newborn babe:around him,eyes
– gifted with every keener appetite
than mere unmiracle can quite appease –
humbly in their imagined bodies kneel
(over time space doom dream while floats the whole

perhapsless mystery of paradise)

mind without soul may blast some universe
to might have been,and stop ten thousand stars
but not one heartbeat of this child;nor shall
even prevail a million questionings
against the silence of his mother's smile

– whose only secret all creation sings

E.E. Cummings

BIRTH

Oh, fields of wonder
Out of which
Stars are born.
And moon and sun
And me as well,
Like stroke
Of lightning
In the night
Some mark
To make
Some word
To tell.

Langston Hughes

BORN YESTERDAY

Tightly-folded bud,
I have wished you something
None of the others would:
Not the usual stuff
About being beautiful,
Or running off a spring
Of innocence and love –
They will all wish you that,
And should it prove possible,
Well, you're a lucky girl.

But if it shouldn't, then
May you be ordinary;
Have, like other women,
An average of talents:
Not ugly, not good-looking,
Nothing uncustomary
To pull you off your balance,
That, unworkable itself,
Stops all the rest from working.
In fact, may you be dull –
If that is what a skilled,
Vigilant, flexible,
Unemphasised, enthralled
Catching of happiness is called.

Philip Larkin

The coming of a child into the family circle widens its dimensions far beyond the simple addition of another member.

It brings the miracle of a new personality struggling for its own fulfilment. Therefore, it is quite natural for us to be thrilled at the sight of new births.

However, as the years pass it is too easy to take our children for granted. Whatever their ages they deserve the tender love and firm guidance, which only we as parents, teachers and friends can give.

Moreover, these children have a right to a faith in themselves, in the story of mankind, in their particular heritage, and in the vast universe-home which is theirs.

It is to symbolize these possibilities and responsibilities that we have come to this ceremony.

David H. MacPherson

Behold the child, the visitor. He has come from nowhere, for he was not before this, and it is nowhere that he goes, wherefore he is called a visitor, for the visitor is one who comes from the unknown to stay but awhile and then to the unknown passes on again.

The child has come forth out of the great womb of the earth. The child has come forth to stand with star dust in his hair, with the rush of planets in his blood, his heart beating out the seasons of eternity, with a shining in his eyes like the sunlight, with hands to shape with that same force that shaped him out of the raw stuff of the universe.

When one baby is born it is the symbol of all birth and life, and therefore all men must rejoice and smile, and all men must lose their hearts to a child.

Kenneth L. Patton – from *Man Is the Meaning*

This mannikin who just now
Broke prison and stepped free
Into his own identity –
Hand, foot and brow
A finished work, a breathing miniature –
Was still, one night ago
A hope, a dread, a mere shape we
Had lived with, only sure
Something would grow
Out of its coiled nine-months nonentity.

... How like a blank sheet
His lineaments appear;
But there's invisible writing here
Which the day's heat
Will show: legends older than language, glum
Histories of the tribe,
Directives from his near and dear –
Charms, curses, rules of thumb –
He will transcribe
Into his own blood to write upon an heir.

... Welcome to earth, my child!

... We time-worn folk renew
Ourselves at your enchanted spring,
As though mankind's begun
Again in you.

C. Day Lewis from – 'The Newborn'

RIDERS

The surest thing there is is we are riders,
And though none too successful at it, guiders,
Through everything presented, land and tide
And now the very air, of what we ride.

What is this talked-of mystery of birth
But being mounted bareback on the earth?
We can just see the infant up astride,
His small fist buried in the busy hide.

There is our wildest mount – the headless horse.
But though it runs unbridled off its course,
And all our blandishments would seem defied,
We have ideas yet that we haven't tried.

Robert Frost

Go, and be happy
You are born into the dazzling light of day

Go, and be wise
You are born upon an earth which needs new eyes

Go, and be strong
You are born into a world where love rights wrong

Go, and be brave
Possess your soul; that you alone can save

Siegfried Sassoon

EVOLUTION

Out of the dusk a shadow,
Then a spark:
Out of the cloud a silence,
Then a lark:
Out of the heart a rapture,
Then, a pain:
Out of the dead cold ashes,
Life again.

John B. Tabb

THE LITTLE PEOPLE

A dreary place would this earth be
Were there no little people in it;
The song of life would lose its mirth,
Were there no children to begin it;

No forms, like buds to grow,
And make the admiring heart surrender;
No little hands on breast and brow,
To keep the thrilling love chords tender.

The sterner souls would grow more stern,
Unfeeling nature more inhuman,
And man to stoic coldness turn,
And woman would be less than woman.

Life's song indeed would lose its charm,
   were there no babies to begin it;
A doleful place this world would be
   were there no little people in it.

     John Greenleaf Whittier

WOMAN TO CHILD

You who were darkness warmed my flesh
where out of darkness rose the seed.
Then all a world I made in me;
all the world you hear and see
hung upon my dreaming blood.

There moved the multitudinous stars,
and coloured birds and fishes moved.
There swam the sliding continents.
All time lay rolled in me, and sense,
and love that knew not its beloved.

O node and focus of the world;
I hold you deep within that well
you shall escape and not escape –
that mirrors still your sleeping shape;
that nurtures still your crescent cell.

I wither and you break from me;
yet though you dance in living light
I am the earth, I am the root,
I am the stem that fed the fruit,
the link that joins you to the night.

Judith Wright

CHILDREN

ON THE SEASHORE

On the seashore of endless worlds children meet.

The infinite sky is motionless overhead and the restless water is boisterous. On the seashore of endless worlds the children meet with shouts and dances.

They build their houses with sand, and they play with empty shells. With withered leaves they weave their boats and smilingly float them on the vast deep. Children have their play on the seashore of worlds.

They know not how to swim, they know not how to cast nets. Pearl-fishers dive for pearls, merchants sail in their ships, while children gather pebbles and scatter them again. They seek not for hidden treasures, they know not how to cast nets.

The sea surges up with laughter, and pale gleams the smile of the sea-beach... on the seashore of endless worlds is the great meeting of children.

Rabindranath Tagore

The spirits of children are remote and wise,
They must go free
Like fishes in the sea
Or starlings in the skies,
Whilst you remain
The shore where they can lightly come again...

Frances Cornford – from 'Ode on the whole duty
of Parents'

THE WOMAN WITH THE BABY
TO THE PHILOSOPHER

How can I dread you, O portentous wise,
When I consider you were once this size?
How cringe before the sage who understands,
Who once had foolish, perfect, waving hands,
As small as these are? How bow down in dread,
When I conceive your warm, domed, downy head
Smelling of soap? O you – from North to South
Renowned – who put your toes inside your mouth.

Frances Cornford

LEARNING TO TALK

See this small one, tiptoe on
The green foothills of the years,
Views a younger world than yours;
When you go down, he'll be the tall one.

Dawn's dew is on his tongue –
No word for what's behind the sky,
Naming all that meets the eye,
Pleased with sunlight over a lawn.

Hear his laughter. He can't contain
The exquisite moment overflowing.
Limbs leaping, woodpecker flying
Are for him and not hereafter.

Tongue trips, recovers, triumphs,
Turning all ways to express
What the forward eye can guess –
That time is his and earth young.

We are growing too like trees
To give the rising wind a voice:
Eagles shall build upon our verse,
Our winged seed are tomorrow's sowing.

Yes, we learn to speak for all
Whose hearts here are not at home,
All who march to a better time
And breed the world for which they burn.

Though we fall once, though we often,
Though we fall to rise not again,
From our horizon sons begin;
When we go down, they will be tall ones.

C. Day Lewis

Nothing is strange to a child for whom
   everything is new.
Where all things are new nothing is novel.
The child does not yet know what belongs and
   what does not;
therefore for him all things belong.
The ear of a child is open to all music.
His eyes are open to all arts.
His mind is open to all tongues.
His being is open to all manners.
In the child's country there are no foreigners.

Kenneth L. Patton – from *This World, My Home*

THE ZULU GIRL

When in the sun the red hot acres smoulder,
Down where the sweating gang its labour plies,
A girl flings down her hoe, and from her shoulder
Unslings her child tormented by the flies.

She takes him to a ring of shadow pooled
By thorn-trees: purpled with the blood of ticks,
While her sharp nails, in slow caresses ruled,
Prowl through his hair with sharp electric clicks.

His sleepy mouth plugged by the heavy nipple,
Tugs like a puppy, grunting as he feeds:
Through his frail nerves her own deep languors ripple
Like a broad river sighing through its reeds.

Yet in that drowsy stream his flesh imbibes
An old unquenched unsmotherable heat –
The curbed ferocity of beaten tribes,
The sullen dignity of their defeat.

Her body looms above him like a hill
Within whose shade a village lies at rest,
Or the first cloud so terrible and still
That bears the coming harvest in its breast.

Roy Campbell

THE FUTURE

A WISH FOR MY CHILDREN

On this doorstep I stand
year after year
to watch you going

and think: May you not
skin your knees. May you
not catch your fingers
in car doors. May
your hearts not break,

May tide and weather
wait for your coming

and may you grow strong
to break
all webs of my weaving.

Evangeline Paterson

I HAVE SEEN...

I have seen a mother at a cot – so I know what love is;

I have looked into the eyes of a child – so I know what
faith is;

I have seen a rainbow – so I know what beauty is;

I have felt the pounding of the sea – so I know what
power is;

I have planted a tree – so I know what hope is;

I have heard a wild bird sing – so I know what freedom is;

I have seen a chrysalis burst into life – so I know what
mystery is;

I have lost a friend – so I know what sorrow is;

I have seen a star-decked sky – so I know what infinite is;

I have seen and felt all these things – so I know what life is.

Anon

THE GIFT

I want to give you something, my child,
for we are drifting in the stream of the world.

Our lives will be carried apart, and our love forgotten.

But I am not so foolish as to hope that I could buy your heart with my gifts.

Young is your life, your path long, and you drink the love we bring you at one draught and turn and run away from us.

You have your play and your playmates. What harm is there if you have no time or thought for us?

We, indeed, have leisure enough in old age to count the days that are past, to cherish in our hearts what our hands have lost for ever.

The river runs swift with a song, breaking through all barriers. But the mountain stays and remembers, and follows her with his love.

Rabindranath Tagore

For the gift of childhood, whose innocence and laughter keep the world young, we all rejoice and give thanks. May this sweet life, which we have accepted into our community of ideals and friendship, receive abundantly the blessings of health, love, knowledge and wisdom, and in its turn give back richly to the common heritage that endures from generation to generation.

Anon

We are mindful that within each child there exists an immense potential that emerges as the years pass – and we realize with some apprehension that the quality of our own lives will determine how well this potential is realized in full bloom and flower. On this day of great promise, we dedicate ourselves to the children here presented, and to all children.

Fred A. Cappuccino

Let our children learn to be honest, both with themselves and with all others. This is a basic human value.

Let our children learn to love truth. No matter whence it comes, so it be truth let them freely accept it, even when it goes against them. If they do this, they will not be much hampered by prejudice, for wherever truth can enter, prejudice cannot long remain. Moreover, by fidelity to truth the mind is nourished and becomes well grown.

Let our children find courage and discover that they are stronger than the things of which they are afraid. Courage in their dealings with their own lives, courage in speaking out for the right, in condemning injustice, in standing for good against evil, courage to remain loyal to a deep conviction at whatever cost.

Let our children cultivate breadth of humanity: a cordial welcome... for whatever is beneficial to the human race no matter whence it comes.

Let our children cultivate kindness, for it does not often come without cultivation, and it is needed: the world is too harsh.

Let our children cultivate humility. Let our children learn that they are like other people... and that there is good and bad in all of us, and that each of us must make a hard struggle to bring the good out on top. Then, because of their own lost battles, they will acquire a gentle wisdom and walk softly where other people might get hurt.

A. Powell Davies

For the gift of childhood and its family setting in our lives, we lift up grateful hearts. Though we cannot save them from trial or danger, we would, by example and encouragement, help them to find courage, wisdom, and love in our midst. We would learn from them as they experience the days of their years with us, and we shall welcome the day when they shall stand among us challenging us and offering a new companionship.

Donald Johnston

What have I got exactly? And what am I going to do with her? And what for that matter will she do with me? I have got a daughter, whose life is already separate from mine, whose will already follows its own directions, and who has quickly corrected my woolly preconceptions of her being something remorselessly different. She is the child of herself and will be what she is. I am merely the keeper of her temporary helplessness. Even so, with luck, she can alter me; indeed, is doing so now. At this stage in my life she will give me more than she gets, and may even later become my keeper. But if I could teach her anything at all – by unloading upon her some of the ill-tied parcels of my years – I'd like it to be acceptance and a relish for life.

What I want for my child is an important beginning, a background where she can most naturally grow. My own background was rough, but it was a good time too, and I want her to have one like it. I was lucky to be raised in a country district, rich with unpackaged and unpriced rewards; and although we were materially poor I believe there are worse things than that kind of poverty. So I would like to give my child chances to be surprised, periods of waiting to sharpen her longings, then some treat or treasure that was worth looking forward to, and an interval to enjoy and remember it.

Given this world to be in, where she can grow reasonably wild, she will also expect the comfort of some authority. To load any child with absolute freedom is to force it to inhabit a wasteland, where it must push its will to find the limits allowed it and grow frantic unless it does. Let her have the assurance, then, of a proper authority, and of a not too inflexible routine, within whose restraints she may take occasional refuge – otherwise I hope she'll be free. I want her to be free from fear to enquire and get answers, free to imagine and tell tall tales, free to be curious and to show enthusiasm, and free at times to invade my silences.

Laurie Lee – from *The Firstborn*

'If a child lives with tolerance, he learns to be patient;
If a child lives with encouragement, he learns confidence;
If a child lives with praise, he learns to appreciate;
If a child lives with fairness, he learns judgement;
If a child lives with acceptance and friendship, he learns to give love to the world.'

adapted from Dorothy Law Nolte

… Your children are not your children.
They are the sons and daughters of Life's
      longing for itself.
They come through you but not from you,
And though they are with you yet they
      belong not to you.

You may give them your love
      but not your thoughts.
For their souls dwell in the house of tomorrow,
which you cannot visit, not even in your dreams.
You may strive to be like them,
      but seek not to make them like you.
For life goes not backward nor tarries with yesterday.
You are the bows from which your children
as living arrows are sent forth.

> Kahlil Gibran from *The Prophet*

... May she be granted beauty and yet not
Beauty to make a stranger's eye distraught,
Or hers before a looking-glass, for such,
Being made beautiful overmuch,
Consider beauty a sufficient end,
Lose natural kindness and maybe
The heart-revealing intimacy
That chooses right, and never find a friend.

... May she become a flourishing hidden tree,
That all her thoughts may like the linnet be,
And have no business but dispensing round
Their magnanimities of sound,
Nor but in merriment begin a chase,
Nor but in merriment a quarrel.
O may she live like some green laurel
Rooted in one dear perpetual place.

... And may her bridegroom bring her to a house
Where all's accustomed, ceremonious;
For arrogance and hatred are the wares
Peddled in the thoroughfares.
How but in custom and in ceremony
Are innocence and beauty born?
Ceremony's a name for the rich horn,
And custom for the spreading laurel tree.

W. B. Yeats from 'A Prayer for my Daughter'

Now this is the day.
Our child,
Into the daylight
You will go out standing.
Preparing for your day.

Our child, it is your day,
This day.
May your road be fulfilled.
In your thoughts may we live,
May we be the ones whom your thoughts will embrace,
May you help us all to finish our roads.

From the Writings of the Zuni Indians

SUGGESTED ADDITIONAL READINGS

No anthology can be complete or cater for all readers' tastes. We list here a number of additional poems which we could not include in this collection. They are all readily accessible in widely used anthologies or in the collected works of the authors.

Funerals
Lionel Abrahams – Agnostic's Funeral Prayer
Maya Angelou – Ailey, Baldwin, Floyd, Killens, and Mayfield
W.H. Auden – 'Stop all the clocks, cut off the telephone ...' (*Twelve Songs, IX*)
Hilaire Belloc – My Own Country
George Gordon Noel, Lord Byron – So, We'll Go No More A-Roving
John Clare – 'Love lies beyond the tomb ...'
W.H. Davies – Leisure ('What is this life if full of care ...')
Walter de la Mare – England
Max Ehrhart – Desiderata
Emily Dickinson – Because I Could Not Stop for Death
T.S. Eliot – 'We shall not cease from exploration...' (from conclusion of Little Gidding, in *Four Quartets*)
T.S. Eliot – 'In the beginning is my end ...' (from East Coker, in *Four Quartets*)
James Fenton – I Know What I'm Missing
Robert Frost – The Silken Tent
Thom Gunn – My Sad Captains
Seamus Heaney – The Wishing Tree

W.E. Henley – Margaritae Sorori, I.M.

A.E. Housman – 'From far, from eve to morning ...' (A Shropshire Lad XXXII)

Sarah Jack – 'Dull now the ache that rocks me ...' – from the poem Coming To Terms

Rudyard Kipling – If

Philip Larkin – Days; An Arundel Tomb

John Lennon – (song lyrics) Imagine

Louis MacNeice – The Sunlight on the Garden

John Gillespie Magee – High Flight (An Airman's Ecstasy)

Leo Marks – Code Poem for the French Resistance – for Violet Szabo

John Masefield – Sea Fever

Edna O'Brien – A Poem (When the blinds are down)

Coventry Patmore – 'Too soon, too soon comes death to show ...'

Marjorie Pizer – The Existence of Love

P.B. Shelley – Ozymandias

Stevie Smith – Not Waving but Drowning

William Shakespeare – 'Fear no more the heat o' the sun ...' (Cymbeline)

William Shakespeare – Sonnet 60 ('Like as the waves that make towards the pebbled shore ...')

William Shakespeare – The Seven Ages of Man (As You Like It)

Edna St Vincent Millay – 'Time does not bring relief; you have lied ...'

R.L. Stevenson – Requiem

Alfred, Lord Tennyson – Crossing The Bar

Dylan Thomas – Do not go gentle into that good night

Weddings
Ann Bradstreet – To My Dear and Loving Husband
T.S. Eliot – To My Wife
Gloria Fuertes – When I Hear Your Name
Seamus Heaney – Scaffolding
Adrian Henri – Without You
Christopher Marlowe – The Passionate Shepherd to his Love
Ogden Nash – Tin Wedding Whistle
Theodore Roethke – Wish for a Young Wife
Bruce Springsteen – (song lyrics) If I Should Fall Behind

Namings
Eugene Field – Wynken, Blynken, and Nod
Sylvia Plath – Morning Song

Readers who can offer suitable material for any of the above categories are encouraged to send it to the British Humanist Association, for possible inclusion in a further published anthology, to the following address:

BHA
Bradlaugh House
47 Theobald's Road
London
WC1X 8SP

AUTHORS' INDEX

FIRST LINE INDEX